"With wealth concen

polls show broad support for a wealth tax but lots of opposition from the elite. This easy-to-read book explains why. Share the Wealth makes a compelling and convincing case that Canadians would benefit enormously from an end to 'wealth hoarding' in Canada."

—Linda McQuaig, author of *The Sport & Prey of Capitalists*

"How will government's raise revenues to pay for improved public goods and services in a post-COVID-19 economy? There is a broad policy consensus that a more sustainable, resilient and inclusive economy will require a more progressive approach to income and wealth taxes. Gauvin and MacEwen have done an excellent job summarizing the literature and arguments. Read this book."

—Kevin Page, President of the Institute of Fiscal Studies and Democracy, University of Ottawa, Former Parliamentary Budget Officer of Canada

"Gauvin and MacEwen believe that we do not have to live in a Canada where those at the top get growing incomes and lower taxes, while everyone else puts up with income stagnation and public service cuts. The inequality of COVID-19's impacts only heightens the urgency of their proposals for fairer taxes and better policies. A book that deserves to be widely read."

—Lars Osberg, Professor of Economics at Dalhousie University, author of *The Age of Increasing Inequality*, former president of the Canadian Economics Association

"The authors show how a series of tax cuts favouring the rich and corporations by governments, from Jean Chrétien and Paul Martin to Stephen Harper, left us with great inequality and $50 billion a year short to fund needed social programs. Their analysis shows precisely how the tax system favors the rich at the expense of the rest of us. And they provide solutions! A splendid book."

—Ed Broadbent, chair of the Broadbent Institute and former leader of the NDP

"A timely exploration of the most troubling economic fallout of the pandemic, tackling myths and proposing solutions with rigour."

—Heather Scoffield, *Toronto Star* economics columnist and Ottawa Bureau Chief

"Share the Wealth details the consequences of inequality and shreds common propaganda against wealth and corporate taxes in this accessible guide on why these taxes are necessary — urgent, even, especially in the shadow of COVID-19 — to transform Canada into a healthier, kinder and fairer nation."

—Meghan Bell, author of "I'm Part of the 0.1 Percent and I Want a Wealth Tax" in *The Walrus*

SHARE THE WEALTH!

SHARE THE WEALTH!

How we can tax Canada's super-rich and create a better country for everyone

JONATHAN GAUVIN AND ANGELLA MacEWEN

JAMES LORIMER & COMPANY LTD., PUBLISHERS
TORONTO

James Lorimer & Company Ltd., Publishers acknowledges funding support from the Ontario Arts Council (OAC), an agency of the Government of Ontario. We acknowledge the support of the Canada Council for the Arts, which last year invested $153 million to bring the arts to Canadians throughout the country. This project has been made possible in part by the Government of Canada and with the support of Ontario Creates.

Cover design: Tyler Cleroux

Library and Archives Canada Cataloguing in Publication

Title: Share the wealth! : how we can tax Canada's super-rich and create a better country for everyone / Jonathan Gauvin and Angella MacEwen.
Names: Gauvin, Jonathan, author. | MacEwen, Angella, author.
Description: Includes bibliographical references and index.
Identifiers: Canadiana (print) 20210174609 | Canadiana (ebook) 20210174897 | ISBN 9781459416567 (softcover) | ISBN 9781459416574 (EPUB)
Subjects: LCSH: Income distribution—Canada. | LCSH: Rich people—Taxation—Canada. | LCSH: Corporations—Taxation—Canada. | LCSH: Wealth tax—Canada.
Classification: LCC HC120.I5 G39 2021 | DDC 336.20086/210971—dc23

Published by:
James Lorimer & Company Ltd., Publishers
117 Peter Street, Suite 304
Toronto, ON, Canada
M5V 0M3
www.lorimer.ca

Printed and bound in Canada.

For our children – Anna, Maëva and Matéo

CONTENTS

FOREWORD

It's April 2021 and things are bad.

Let's start with the obvious. We are in the grips of a global COVID-19 pandemic that has had a devastating toll on people in Canada and around the world. People have lost their jobs, small businesses have shut their doors without knowing if they will ever open again, and many people, particularly seniors living in long-term care, have lost their lives.

But that's not all. COVID-19 has dramatically exposed pre-existing problems in our healthcare system, long-term care, our social safety net, and our economy at large.

On top of that, the global pandemic isn't the only crisis we are facing.

When I was a kid growing up with science fiction books and movies that imagined the future, I had a completely different picture of what 2021 would look like.

I thought the dystopic movies and novels about post-apocalyptic worlds where human survivors of environmental catastrophe roamed a ravaged earth would surely motivate society to solve the climate crisis.

I thought the countless example of corporate greed and excess throughout the '80s, '90s, and early 2000s, where the economy benefited a select few at the very top, would surely encourage us to build a sustainable economy that guaranteed shared prosperity for all.

I thought all the painful and traumatic incidents of racial injustice, particularly anti-Indigenous and anti-Black, would surely spur society to finally put an end to hate and systemic racism.

Sadly, I was wrong.

If anything, these problems have worsened. The climate crisis continues to rage. Hate and hate crimes are on the rise while systemic racism continues to oppress racialized people, especially

Indigenous and Black people. The economy continues to concentrate wealth in the hands of the super-rich to the detriment of everyone else.

Young people for the first time worry that they will have fewer opportunities than their parents to get a good job, own a home, or raise a family. More and more families live on the brink, one paycheque away from losing it all. Seniors who should retire in dignity after a life of hard work often have to choose between buying food or medication.

In the midst of this struggle, the economy, despite some ups and downs, continues to post record levels of growth and wealth. But none of it seems to make it to the actual people driving the economy.

While people struggle, the super-rich continue to amass wealth. Economic inequality has created a yawning chasm between everyday people and the super-wealthy.

So yes, things are bad.

But I'm an optimist. Not just any kind of optimist — I am a defiant optimist. I have internalized my mom's teaching of "Chardi Kala" or "Rising Spirits" in the face of hopeless odds. My science and legal education forces me to pay close attention to the facts. So my optimism does not come at the cost of denying the reality. I'm an optimist because I maintain, against the odds, a powerful belief that we can turn things around.

This system didn't just happen. It was made by design. In Canada for example, previous federal governments both Liberal and Conservative purposely made laws that rigged the system in favour of the ultra-rich at the cost of everyday people.

But here's the thing.

If choices made by previous governments rigged the system, that means we can make different choices to obtain different results. Instead of a system that continues to benefit the ultra-rich and hurt everyone else, we can design a system that creates shared prosperity for all.

I believe we are all connected. That when people around us are suffering we are all directly affected. When we hurt the planet we are hurting ourselves. As leader of the New Democratic Party I am committed to building a sustainable economy, one that creates shared prosperity for all while protecting the planet we call home. I believe we will all benefit from a society free from systemic racism and hate. I am committed to building a world where we lift each other up so that we all rise together.

In this book Jonathan and Angella show us how we can start building toward that world. They demonstrate how building a brighter future is not only possible but achievable with different priorities, and most importantly, different choices.

Jonathan and Angella show the surprising depth of economic inequality in Canada and document how decades of tax cuts have allowed the super-rich to hoard wealth while leaving little for the rest of us.

They make a convincing case that the solution is to tax the super-rich, and in the second part of the book they paint in vivid and clear colors how it can be done.

In the end, they present a hopeful vision of the future where the economy is more fair and we take better care of each other.

This is the future that New Democrats are working towards, a future where we lift each other so that we all rise together.

— Jagmeet Singh, leader of the NDP, April 7, 2021

AUTHORS' PREFACE

In the middle of December 2020, I got a text from my friend Jonathan Gauvin, asking if I had time to chat about "an interesting project." Since Jonathan worked for the NDP, I expected that it might have something to do with his work there. I thought maybe it would be related to tax policy, since I had recently participated in a press conference with NDP Leader Jagmeet Singh talking through the details of wealth taxes.

I was right on those two counts, but unprepared for the scale of Jonathan's proposed project – that we write a book together on taxing the rich. He had been talking to an interested publisher and thought that if we worked together, we could have a first draft done in six weeks. (It took us a little bit longer.)

Jonathan had done a lot of research on federal tax policy and knew the political state of play inside and out. I would provide the context for exactly how extreme economic inequality is in Canada and how tax fairness is part of a broader way of thinking about the economy differently. Together we could flesh out a social democratic vision for the federal government's role in shaping a more equitable economy.

I was excited. As an economist for a trade union, I work on issues related to economic inequality every day. Whether it's about stagnant wages for workers, employers outsourcing work to precarious temporary contractors, or privatization and underfunding of public services, I keep coming back to the same root problem – the rules are rigged against most of us. Policy-makers relying on a flawed understanding of how the economy works tinker around the edges of social and economic policy while leaving structural issues intact.

Around the world, activists and academics have been thinking about how to make the economy work for the rest of us, not just the rich and powerful. And even though zombie myths about how the economy works are still widespread, more and more people are rejecting them in favour of different ideas. Economists are questioning long-held beliefs and proposing new models – from how money and government debt work to how race and class intersect to create economic inequality.

In our different roles, we've been thinking about these ideas too and how they apply to Canada. How much has wealth and income inequality grown here and how has it happened? What would we need to change in order to get a fairer economy?

This book is our answer to those questions. It's a practical guide to building the foundation for a prosperous and equitable society. Taxing the rich is only the first part of the solution. We must also shift our understanding of how the economy works and what the government's role is in creating wealth.

"Share the wealth" isn't a request; it's a prescription for an ailing economy.

—A.M.

Coming from a disadvantaged background and having to overcome many challenges that came with it, I have seen the costs of inequality up close. Like many Canadians, I know what it is like to have to miss meals and proper dental care because of insufficient income, to have to move because the rent has not been paid or the electricity has been turned off. I have seen firsthand the impacts of addiction as well as mental health issues. I have also lived and seen the impacts of the lack of services and support for those who need them. I am very familiar with anguish, suffering, hopelessness and grief, but also with love, acceptance, compassion and hope. If I have been able to overcome these challenges early on, it is mainly because I have met some incredible people along the way who have helped me in many different ways. My personal experiences, my education and my professional career have solidified my belief that we are always better off taking care of each other than being left to our own devices. I believe in the power of collectives and in gathering our strengths to better support each other.

After working on Parliament Hill for several years, I have seen the backstage of power and government decision-making.

Nothing really surprised me, except one aspect – the recurrence of scientific reports on the impacts of economic inequality on our society that make waves for a day, sometimes two, before they are promptly forgotten. Just like the climate crisis, experts keep saying that if we don't address inequality, the consequences will be very serious for all of us. The parties that have been in power will say they agree, but their actions remain symbolic, surface-level and do not solve the problems identified. I wanted to participate in this book with Angella because I believe that as a society, we have the power and the responsibility to do better. With our busy lives we don't always have time to stay informed and sometimes we don't know where to start. I wanted to help spread the facts about inequality in Canada, to dispel some of the myths that accompany them, but most importantly to offer concrete and viable actions to address it. What can you do as an individual who cares, what can we do as a community that cares, what can we do as elected officials who care? I wanted to help mobilize people for a cause that I believe is central to many of the problems facing us. I know we need to get more elected people who give a voice to those who lack one. Having had a front-row seat to the cross-party negotiations for COVID-19 assistance, I have seen the impacts of elected officials who truly have the interests of the people at heart. I have seen the government wanting to do the bare minimum while other elected officials across the aisle fought for more help. I have seen the power that the economic elite has over political decision-making and rather than being discouraged I have become even more motivated to change the system. COVID-19 demonstrated that when the government prioritizes something, action can be quick and meaningful. In working on this book, I hope to mobilize people to fight against economic inequality in a similar way we fought against COVID-19. It's a different "virus," but it has just as much impact. Written with my precious children in mind, *Share the Wealth* is a part of the solution I wish to see in Canada and I know that together, we can do it and be that change.

—J.G.

PART ONE:
CHOICES AND CONSEQUENCES

CHAPTER 1

AN ECONOMY THAT WORKS — FOR THE WEALTHY

The super-wealthy have everything they could ask for. Internationally, their global power and influence have enabled them to concentrate corporate ownership, reap record profits, keep workers' wages low and pay less tax than they did thirty years ago. Canada is no exception.

The current state of affairs is not an accident; it stems directly from political decisions and an economic system designed to benefit the wealthiest among us. Since the 1980s, governments around the world have reduced taxes on corporate profits and personal wealth, weakened regulations and privatized public infrastructure. These decisions allow the powerful to hoard wealth at the expense of workers, consumers, the environment and social cohesion.

Economic inequality is not just unfair; it also creates a deeply dysfunctional economy. The more those at the top make decisions based on increasing their own wealth rather than our shared wealth, the less the economy can perform its role of sustaining people and our societies.

In this chapter, we demonstrate the inequality of both income and wealth in Canada, noting that income inequality and wealth inequality are different but connected. Wealth constitutes the single most important factor determining who has access to opportunities and influence in Canada. By understanding how people get rich and stay rich, we can learn how to change the rules of the game to make it fairer for everyone.

The Rise of Income and Wealth Inequalities — Globally

The rise of income and wealth inequality around the world is well documented. Every year the numbers get worse — or better, depending on your perspective.

Between 2017 and 2018, a new billionaire was created every two days.[1]

Furthermore, billionaires have more wealth than ever before. From 2017 to 2020, the average billionaire's fortune swelled by 4.2 billion USD, creating the greatest concentration of wealth since the U.S. Gilded Age at the turn of the twentieth century.[2]

Four billion is a very large number, and it's tough to visualize exactly how much money $4.2 billion represents. One way to put it in perspective is to think about how much money you would have to earn each year of your working life to get there. If you started working full-time when you were eighteen and retired at sixty, you'd have to be making a tax-free salary of $100 million every year to have earned $4.2 billion. Our "average billionaire" was able to accumulate this much additional wealth in just three years.

A report published by Oxfam in 2019 showed that the wealth of the world's billionaires increased by $900 billion USD in 2018 — the equivalent of $2.5 billion a day. During the same period, the wealth of the poorest half of humanity (3.8 billion people) fell by 11 per cent.[3]

According to the Oxfam report, "the world's richest man, Jeff Bezos, owner of Amazon, saw his fortune increase to $112 billion USD. Just 1% of his fortune is the equivalent to the whole health budget for Ethiopia, a country of 105 million people."[4]

Think about that for a minute: one man could pay a 1 per cent annual wealth tax and double the health budget for a nation of 105 million people.

The extreme wealth of the lucky few sits in stark contrast with the 3.4 billion people around the world subsisting on less than $5.50 a day — and the COVID-19 pandemic did not help. On the contrary, the pandemic showed us that we are most definitely *not* in this together.

While eleven million Americans remained unemployed in December 2020, Jeff Bezos had nearly doubled his net worth from before the pandemic to over $200 billion.[5] Elon Musk had nearly quadrupled his net worth from $24.6 billion USD before the pandemic to over $92.8 billion USD in October 2020.[6]

Between April and July 2020, billionaires around the world increased their wealth by more than a quarter (27.5 per cent), just as millions of people lost their jobs or struggled to get by.[7] Many of the workers who continued to go to work in person and did the literal heavy lifting that generated this wealth did so without wage increases, paid job-protected sick days, or adequate health and safety protection.

The World Bank predicts that COVID-19 will continue to increase inequality globally, "potentially bringing the total number of new people living in extreme poverty to between 110 million and 150 million."[8]

The Rise of Income and Wealth Inequalities — in Canada

We Canadians often think these global trends don't apply to us. As a country, we tend to compare ourselves to the US, which is a pretty low bar if we are being honest. The reality is that while we might be doing slightly better than the worst, we have no reason to be smug.

The Parliamentary Budget Officer (PBO) is the independent expert who provides nonpartisan information and analysis regarding the economy to parliamentarians in Ottawa. The PBO estimated that in 2016, Canada's top one per cent held one-quarter of all the wealth in Canada — a total value of $3.1 trillion CAD.[9] This is an extreme concentration of wealth that only gets more extreme upon closer examination.

David Macdonald, a senior economist with the Canadian Centre for Policy Alternatives, a think-tank funded by labour unions and individual Canadians — but not corporations — took an in-depth look at wealth concentration in Canada. He found that the eighty-seven wealthiest families had net wealth of $259 billion in 2016. To put this in perspective, this equals the combined net wealth of the twelve million poorest Canadians — or roughly as much as the collective wealth of everyone living in Newfoundland and Labrador, New Brunswick and Prince Edward Island.[10]

Macdonald's research also revealed what we all know — that the rich keep getting richer. Between 2012 and 2016, the average wealth of those eighty-seven families rose from $2.2 billion to $3.0 billion — an increase of 37 per cent — while the net worth of middle-class families in Canada only increased by 16 per cent.[11]

As we have seen around the world, the pandemic only made the gap between the wealthy and the rest of us more extreme. $78 billion richer during the first year of the COVID-19 pandemic.[12] Not a single one of the top twenty billionaires in Canada suffered a decrease in their overall wealth between the emergence of COVID-19 and the end of 2020.[13]

Between March 18 and December 31, 2020, Tobi Lutke, CEO of Canada's most successful tech company to date, Shopify, more than doubled his wealth to over $15 billion. Chip Wilson, Vancouver real estate investor and Lululemon founder, saw his fortune increase by $2.8 billion to nearly $7 billion. James Irving of the Irving family — whose companies include Irving Oil, the shipyard building Canada's new navy ships and the newspapers that serve New Brunswick — saw an increase of $2.4 billion.[14]

Members of Canada's super-wealthy families don't just inherit wealth — some of them inherit extremely well-paid CEO positions.

Macdonald's research on wealth concentration found that among the twenty wealthiest families, nine had relatives on the list of Canada's highest paid CEOs.[15]

For example, ATCO Ltd. is an Alberta-based company that was founded by Donald Southern and his son, Ronald Southern. ATCO and its associated companies have made the Southerns one of the wealthiest families in Canada. According to the company's website, Ronald's daughter, Nancy Southern, has been president and CEO since 2003 and chair of the board of directors since 2012. Nancy was ninety-fourth on the list of the one hundred highest-paid CEOs in 2016.[16] Ronald's other daughter, Linda Southern-Heathcott, is vice-chair of ATCO's board of directors.[17] The Southern family is perhaps better known for founding Spruce Meadows Equestrian Centre outside Calgary and Linda Southern-Heathcott has been the CEO of that enterprise since 2006.[18] This is one of the ways that wealth inequality contributes to growing income inequality.

In terms of *income* inequality, a report from the Canadian Centre for Policy Alternatives showed that by 11:17 a.m. on January 4, 2019, the average top one hundred CEO had already made as much money as the average Canadian worker would make all year.[19] This is no surprise when in recent years, top CEOs made more than two hundred times what an average worker did.

In 2019, the average pay of a top one hundred CEO was $10.8 million, while the average individual income in Canada was $53,482. The minimum salary to be counted among the top one hundred CEOs that year was $6.3 million. Meanwhile, Statistics Canada data from 2018 show that nearly ten million Canadians earned less than $25,000.[20]

We do not have comprehensive information about how much wealth these super-high-income earners hold or how much income the super-wealthy receive from their investments each year. Statistics Canada does publish some data on high-income earners, however, that give us some insight into the relationship between high income and wealth.[21]

Using data from tax filings, we know that the top two thousand income earners in Canada are receiving a greater proportion of their income from wealth than they used to. In 1998, about half their income came from wages and salaries and by 2018 that had fallen to 35 per cent. Statistics Canada does not provide a detailed breakdown of sources for the remainder, but it would largely be from returns on investments — rental incomes, dividends and capital gains. The only solid information we have is the average income from capital gains: the top two thousand income earners — the 0.01 per cent — have seen this amount increase significantly during this time. In 1998, this group's average income from capital gains was just over $600,000 and by 2018 it had risen to over $2 million.[22]

This level of income and wealth inequality has consequences. In 2018, over four million Canadians, including 1.15 million children, were living in homes that struggled to put food on the table[23] — and one in three Canadians acknowledged being very stressed about money most or all of the time.[24] It is also estimated that at least 235,000 Canadians experience homelessness every year[25] and nearly 4.5 million Canadians live in poverty.[26] Beyond that, as of September 2020, there were still more than sixty-one Indigenous communities that did not have access to safe drinking water, many of which had been waiting decades for that basic but essential service.

Income inequality was accelerated by the COVID-19 pandemic. In September 2020, 1.1 million fewer people were employed in Canada compared to pre-COVID-19 levels; another 713,000 workers were technically employed but had lost half or more of their usual hours as a result of the pandemic. Systemic racism and labour market discrimination meant that Black and racialized workers were more likely to lose their employment. By January 2021, the unemployment rate was over 16 per cent for Black workers and 20 per cent for workers who identified as

South Asian, compared to 8.9 per cent for white workers.[27]

COVID-19 amplified pre-existing discrimination. Lower-wage workers were more likely to be exposed to the virus at work and less likely to have paid sick leave than higher wage workers. Indeed, only 25 per cent of workers making less than $25,000 had any paid sick days from their employer. These are workers who could not afford to lose wages. Naturally, systemic racism and labour market discrimination also mean that Black and racialized Canadians are overrepresented among low-wage workers, so they were disproportionately affected by the illness.

If the periods between the first, second and third waves were a predictor of the recovery phase, it seemed clear that lower-income and more vulnerable people would take longer to get back on their feet. British Columbia researchers Alex Hemingway and Michal Rozworski noted that in September 2020, "employment among those making less than $16.03 per hour was still substantially below the pre-pandemic level (87.4%), while the highest wage groups have recovered to pre-pandemic employment levels."[28] As of February 2021, the largest decline in work was among the lowest-wage earners in the country — those with an hourly wage of less than $13.91. As a group, higher-wage earners did not suffer any job losses; instead, this group gained nearly 350,000 jobs during the pandemic.[29]

Every crisis acts as a gas pedal on pre-existing trends, and the pandemic was no different. The income gap was widening before and widened even faster during the pandemic. Some large companies in Canada were fortunate enough to be in a position to profit from COVID-19. Grocery chain owners, for example, increased their wealth by billions of dollars. Not much of this windfall made it to front-line workers, as the main grocery companies had all cancelled their temporary hazard pay benefits for workers by the end of May 2020.

The COVID-19 wage subsidy and other corporate supports put in place by the federal government were also designed in a way that allowed companies to continue hoarding wealth. At least thirty Canadian companies paid out nearly $2 billion in dividends to their shareholders between April and September 2020, all the while receiving millions of dollars in federal government support.[30] For-profit long-term care companies paid out nearly $171 million to shareholders in the first nine months of 2020 at the same time that they received $138.5 million in various government supports — aside from which, for-profit long-term care facilities had higher COVID-19 fatality rates than not-for-profit and public care homes.[31]

Trudeau's federal government had said that it was going to rely on companies to be responsible in their use of federal support rather than attach restrictions as other countries did. This sounds good, but corporations have a responsibility to their shareholders to take advantage of opportunities to increase profits; it's the government's responsibility to make the rules fair.

Where Has Twenty to Thirty Years of Growth Gone?

There is no doubt that in the last thirty years Canada has become a richer country. Its average gross domestic product (GDP) growth has been 2.23 per cent per year and it is the ninth-largest economy in the world. But where did this wealth go? Many people find themselves in a more difficult economic situation than their parents experienced. Housing prices have skyrocketed while wages have stagnated. How can the country be getting wealthier, while most people see nothing of that increase? The chart below helps to answer this question.

While the richest one per cent can count on their wealth to grow (through investment income), any income growth for middle- and working-class people resides almost exclusively in a wage increase. While some of the richest rely on employment income too, the top one per cent of income earners have been able to translate their disproportionate salaries into wealth and increasingly receive significant income from their investment stocks.

Simply put, it would appear that in the last thirty years,

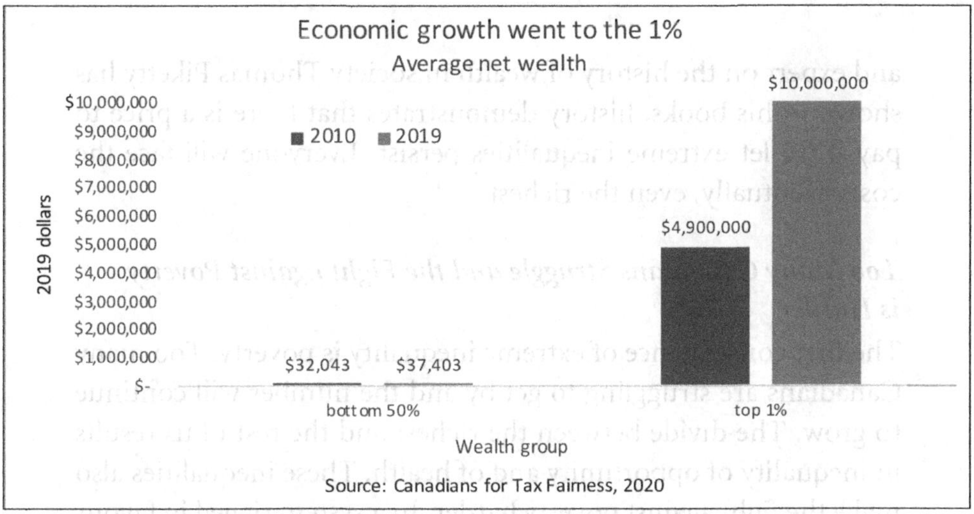

Canada's economic growth has gone into capital growth and considering that capital growth mainly benefits the wealth of the richest one per cent, Canada's economic growth has mainly been in their hands. As Canada's wealth pie has grown over the years, the share of the richest one per cent has increased while that of the 99 per cent has decreased; this led Canada's top one per cent to increase their share of net wealth from 15 per cent in 1999 to 25.7 per cent in 2019.[32]

As we will see a little later, this is the result of successive political decisions that have:

- Given more and more power to big business and the economic elite and less and less to workers.
- Diminished the role of government in distributing wealth equitably.
- Left the country's economic growth mostly in the hands of the richest.

Consequences of Inequality in Canada

Economic and social inequalities have very significant and destructive impacts on society. As the famed French economist and expert on the history of wealth in society Thomas Piketty has shown in his books, history demonstrates that there is a price to pay if we let extreme inequalities persist. Everyone will face the costs eventually, even the richest.

Too Many Canadians Struggle and the Fight against Poverty is Harder

The first consequence of extreme inequality is poverty. Too many Canadians are struggling to get by and the number will continue to grow. The divide between the richest and the rest of us results in inequality of opportunity and of health. These inequalities also make the fight against poverty harder. In a system rigged in favour of people at the top, everyone else has to pay more to cover the shortfall. While the wealthiest are getting richer, Canadians are asked to wait for public services and programs that they need to be healthy, live with dignity and reach their full potential — because governments say they can't afford these services and programs.

As the veteran Canadian economist and public policy analyst Andrew Jackson points out,

> *In all societies, economic inequality underlies important differences in well-being, such as life expectancy. Here in Canada, 65% of men at age 25 will live to age 75, but that varies a lot from 51% for men in the lowest income decile, to 75% for those in the highest income decile. The key point here is that those in the middle do worse than those at the top, so reduced life expectancy is not just a function of poverty. Inequality — a person's relative position in the social hierarchy — matters too.*[33]

In other words, your relative income not only determines how much money you have to spend — it also has a big influence on how long you are likely to live.

One of the best tools we have to fight inequality is universal public services provided by governments, paid for by progressive income taxes. In Canada, public spending on health care, education and other services is among the lowest in the industrialized world — and lower even than it was in the 1990s. Often, the excuse used by successive Conservative and Liberal governments has been that the government does not have enough revenues to maintain or expand public services. As we will explain in more detail later, this is a false argument. Investments in public services are one of the best tools to tackle inequalities, but underfunded public services are also an outcome of existing inequalities.

Investments in public services help the many instead of the few. Underfunded public services have bigger impacts on the working and middle classes than on the one per cent. For example, the richest don't have any problem accessing the medications they need. On the contrary, they are more likely to profit from the skyrocketing price of medications in Canada. But for the rest of us, one in five Canadian households report a family member who in the recent past has not taken a prescribed medicine because of its cost.[34] Almost one million Canadians per year cut back on food or home heating to pay for their medication.[35]

A recent study from the Canadian Federation of Nurses Unions revealed that inadequate drug coverage in Canada leads to hundreds of avoidable, premature deaths annually.[36] HealthCareCAN estimates that between 5.4 and 6.5 per cent of hospital admissions in Canada result from cost-related non-adherence to prescription medication, leading to additional costs of approximately $1.6 billion per year.[37] We all pay the price for the absence of a universal national pharmacare system that would ensure all Canadians free access to the medication they need.

The same is true for dental care in Canada. Oral health is one of the most unequal aspects of health care in Canada because most dental care isn't covered by public insurance plans. This leads 22.4

per cent of Canadians (roughly 6.8 million people) to avoid visiting a dental professional because of cost.

Over one-third of Canadians lack dental insurance.[38] Those without insurance are about three times as likely as those with insurance to avoid seeing a dental professional because of cost. This in turn leads to emergency room visits for dental emergencies, which cost taxpayers at least $155 million annually. Again, we all end up paying for the consequences of unaffordable, untreated dental problems.

There is a long list of other services governments could provide that would give everyone access to what they need at reasonable costs. One is child care services — which cost some Canadians up to $20,000 per child per year. Another is affordable housing. The skyrocketing price of housing has almost half of Canada's millennials thinking that owning a home is just a pipe dream. Renting, the alternative to owning a home, is rapidly growing more expensive too. The increased financialization of rental housing through real estate investment trusts (REITs) has resulted in lower quality and higher cost rental markets. For example, in Toronto, a minimum-wage worker in 2020 had to work a seventy-nine-hour week to afford an average one bedroom apartment and a ninety-six-hour week for a two bedroom apartment.

Those who get left behind face barriers that those at the top of Canada's wage scales are not even aware exist. This is how we get a political class of officials and cabinet ministers that do not even consider helping students amid a pandemic because they think all students can just ask their parents for help.

Problems that are either created or worsened by inequalities are problems we should all want to address because they have consequences for our society as a whole. Inequality is a barrier to upward social mobility in Canada; it means that many young Canadians face the prospect of a worse future than their parents. Parents find it scary to know that their children could be worse off than they were and that many young Canadians will be failed by their country. In this scenario, it is hard to imagine future talented generations being able to achieve their full potential.

Division and Anger

Many economists and historians around the world have warned us that extreme inequalities detrimentally impact the social climate. Some are even worried that we are in a new Gilded Age,[39] evoking the era at the turn of the twentieth century in the US when a few families controlled vast fortunes and the lower classes, fed up with the unfairness built into the system, started to disrupt its functions.[40] The famed American economist, former vice president of the World Bank and Nobel Prize winner Joseph Stiglitz wrote, "For many years, I have been warning that the great divide — the one between the rich and the poor — was not sustainable and that a fairer distribution of income was in the long-run interests of even the rich."[41]

Inequalities, especially when they become so extreme, can lead to political and public anger. Research has shown that in more unequal countries trust is lower,[42] crime is higher,[43] and people are stressed, are less happy and have poorer mental health.[44] Around the world and across Canada, people are starting to say, "Enough." If we don't act to address this reality, we could become more divided and polarized than ever.

As we have seen, some politicians are always ready to channel and fuel that anger to divide us even further. The gap between rich and poor is helping to boost authoritarianism.[45] As a paper published by the international charity Oxfam noted, "Rather than working to heal it, some leaders are instead seeking to vilify immigrants, other ethnic groups, other nations, women and people in poverty."[46]

This frustration even leads some to be more likely to believe in conspiracy theories or to join radical white supremacist groups. We are seeing a rise in hate speech and white supremacy groups threatening our society, our friends and our families. COVID-19 also showed that trust is important in times of crisis and while our governments could have done a better job communicating, we saw thousands of people in Canada believing conspiracy theories about the pandemic and therefore endangering the lives of others by refusing to follow public health advice. If the anger, the fear and the sense of injustice caused by inequalities are not channelled toward a project for a society that is fairer and more inclusive, we will only become more divided and more polarized.

Concentration of Power into the Hands of the Economic Elite

Of course, high levels of wealth and income inequalities lead to massive economic and political power for the few. Many fear that the ever-increasing concentration of wealth — and therefore concentration of power — in the hands of the very rich threatens democracy itself. This is most evident in the US, where there are very few restrictions on financial donations to political parties and candidates and the rich strongly influence media, think tanks and other institutions that help shape public policy.

But we see the same pattern in Canada, reflecting our own social and economic inequalities.[47] The wealthiest influence the two governing federal parties and their decision-making. The few have great influence over how our society is shaped and controlled — from the prices we pay to the services we can offer to the wages we earn.

Excess profits captured by the largest corporations stand as one of the biggest drivers of inequality. Concentrating market power in only a few players has huge consequences on our society and furthers the gap between the richest and the poorest. As Joseph Stiglitz explains,

> *Market power allows firms to exploit consumers by charging higher prices than they otherwise would and by taking advantage of consumers in a variety of other*

> *ways. Higher prices hurt workers just as much as lower wages…*
>
> *Market power also allows firms to exploit workers directly, by paying lower wages than they would otherwise and by taking advantage of labour in other ways. Market power gets translated into political power. The huge profits generated by market power allow corporations to buy influence that further enhances their power and profits, for instance by weakening unions and undermining the enforcement of competition policy, giving free rein to banks to exploit ordinary citizens and structuring globalization in ways that further weakens workers' bargaining power.*[48]

While Stiglitz is talking about the US, we face a similar phenomenon in Canada. Lars Osberg, a leading expert on inequality in Canada and a former president of the Canadian Economics Association, tells us that "the democratic political process is also threatened by the increasing concentration of wealth and economic power in Canada and the political influence of an economic elite whose lifestyles are increasingly disconnected from the realities of ordinary people."[49]

The mechanism for big corporations and economic elites to buy influence in Canada is not as direct as in the US, but it exists and has an enormous impact every day on the policies, decisions and actions of the federal government. The average voter sees little of this activity, but there is an army of lobbyists in Ottawa who spend a lot of time and money trying to influence decision-making.

The voices that legislators hear are overwhelmingly tilted toward the interests of Canada's one per cent, along with giant foreign multinationals like Google, Pfizer, Amazon and Exxon. They certainly get more direct input and pressure from lobbyists speaking for the wealthy and for big business — both Canadian and foreign — than from anyone who has experienced the downside of inequality in Canada. There are also strong social connections between people at the top in Canada and the Liberals and Conservatives. Their members of Parliament are largely drawn from a class of people who never had student loans and never worked jobs without paid sick leave.

Banking, telecommunication, oil and gas, digital platforms and pharmaceutical industries all offer examples of Canadian industries where market power is strong, allowing many to stay at the top by charging high prices, paying low wages and ensuring that governments will not make decisions that could disrupt this highly profitable rent-seeking strategy. "Rent-seeking" is an economic term used to describe firms that make money from leveraging their ownership of scarce resources, existing social connections, or political lobbying; it is often seen in industries with a high concentration of market power. This would be comparable to playing a game of Monopoly where one player begins the game owning half the properties on the board. Such a strategy can guarantee a company high profits, but only at the expense of others.

This is why Canadians are often forced to pay among the highest prices in the world for certain goods and services. Among Organisation for Economic Co-operation and Development (OECD) countries and other developed economies, Canadians pay some of the highest prices for mobile wireless and broadband subscriptions, for example. Consumers in similar countries, like Australia, can pay as little as half as much as Canadians for the same cellphone plan. In 2017, the profits of the "Big Five" telecom companies in Canada totalled $7.49 billion; their profit margins reached an astonishing 38.3 per cent. Market power, high prices and the outsourcing of jobs enabled these massive profits. Using their economic power, telecommunication companies in Canada have often been successful in using their influence to delay political decisions in Ottawa that would increase competition and therefore decrease prices and their market power.

Market power is important, but in our society, the elite who have economic power also have political power, which they use to promote their interests. Canada's one per cent are very successful in influencing decisions by successive Liberal and Conservative governments. For example, in 2015, Justin Trudeau's Liberal party promised to review the stock option loophole. This rule allows rich CEOs to further enrich themselves while avoiding paying income tax on excessive paycheques. After months of pressure from wealthy CEOs, this promise was abandoned.[50]

There has been a similar situation with policies to reduce the high price of drugs in Canada. After promising to review how we regulate the prices of patented drugs, on three separate occasions the Liberals delayed implementing changes that would help Canadians and the health care system generally by reducing drug prices. Why? The delays were caused by industry pressure and intense, successful lobbying. The result has been that millions of people in Canada needlessly continue to pay among the highest prices for pharmaceutical medicines in the world and many remain unable to afford the drugs they need.

Even though public anger with the concentration of power in these industries has grown in recent years, the federal Liberal government did little to address the issue. Budget 2021 continued the practice of shuffling issues off to consultations, making token changes, or ignoring the problem altogether. Many of the budget's measures used public money to provide incentives to the private market, such as expanding the types of equipment and research investments that businesses can write off immediately to lower their taxes. This is an inefficient way to achieve a desired change and does nothing to stop the concentration of power in the hands of a few.

Politicians and governments can always give a reason why the change that was promised does not happen. These reasons are usually faithfully reported by the news media, with little questioning or digging. The typical reasons offered? It's not the right time.

They will just find another way to avoid paying tax. Industry "X" creates a lot of jobs and they can't do that if they must pay tax on profits. Once or twice, we might believe that the proposed change wasn't as beneficial as we had hoped it would be, but there are many other justifications like this. It's not the exception that Liberal and Conservative governments continually side with powerful economic interests instead of siding with the people — it's the rule.

The way the system of government we have in Canada has been designed, the few have way more power and influence than the rest of us. Those with power have no interest in fixing a system that, at least in the short term, will keep serving them extremely well.

Inequality Is Making it Hard to Fight against Sexism, Racism and Climate Change

Beyond economic inequalities, we have other considerable challenges in our country that we need to address. Inequality makes it harder to tackle these issues too.

Every crisis we face affects our society differently, but the common thread is that economic inequality amplifies other forms of discrimination. People with disabilities, women and Black, racialized and Indigenous people are more impacted by income and wealth inequality and rely more on the public services that end up getting squeezed. These groups tend to have greater responsibility for unpaid care, earn less, own less and are more likely to be living in poverty.

As with COVID-19, when a crisis hits, women are the economic shock absorbers — filling the gaps at considerable personal cost. As Oxfam explained in its 2019 report,

> *The economic divide both drives the gap between women and men and is driven by it. Economically unequal countries are countries where women and men are more unequal too. Societies in which the gap between rich and poor is much lower are those in which women are treated more as equals.*[51]

This is also true for Black, racialized and Indigenous people in Canada. If we don't address the big divide between the wealthiest and the rest of us, it will be impossible to get to the bottom of systemic sexism and racism in the country.

The big threat our planet faces is climate change. Like the other challenges already mentioned, the fight against the climate crisis and the inequality crisis are intimately linked. Inequality makes the fight to save our planet from climate breakdown even harder. As Oxfam has shown, the one per cent drove 15 per cent of total world emissions while the bottom 50 per cent generated just 7 per cent of emissions.[52]

We also know that the climate crisis is disproportionately affecting more disadvantaged minority groups. Tim Gore — head of climate policy at Oxfam and a contributing author of the 2020 climate gap report from the United Nations Environment Programme[53] — explains that the data send a clear message:

> *The over-consumption of a wealthy minority is fuelling the climate crisis, yet it is poor communities and young people who are paying the price. It will be practically and politically impossible to close the emissions gap if governments don't cut the carbon footprint of the wealthy and end the inequalities which leave millions of people without access to power or unable to heat their homes.*[54]

Economic inequalities clearly have impacts on the climate crisis. We must tackle them if we truly want to win the war against climate change.

CHAPTER 2

THE MYTHS USED TO CREATE AND JUSTIFY INEQUALITY

Today's economic system, which greatly benefits the richest at the expense of the middle and working classes, is explained by theories developed by some economists about how the economy works — theories that have since been proven false by other economists who have looked at the evidence. These myths continue to be used, however, to thwart any reform of the system. Sometimes, the myths are so strong or have become so deeply rooted in our collective understanding of how economies work that talking to people who believe them is like talking to zombies, as distinguished American economist and Nobel Prize-winner Paul Krugman would say. The data show that those myths are not simply wrong, but also harmful. In this chapter, we will cover the main ones and explain why they are false.

Myth No. 1 — The Market Works Best with No Government Intervention

The first myth, and maybe the most common one, is the theory that the best way to ensure prosperity for everyone is by limiting government intervention and allowing the market to operate unhindered. French economist Thomas Piketty explains the logic of this view as the belief that

> *market forces, individual initiative and productivity growth are the sole determinants of the distribution of income and standard of living, in particular of the least well-off members of society; hence government efforts to redistribute wealth should be limited and should rely on instruments that interfere as little as possible with the virtuous mechanisms of the market.*[1]

This philosophy is sometimes called "laissez-faire economics," from a French term that translates as "let it be." According to laissez-faire economics, markets are the most efficient way to allocate all resources, and any interference with markets and their operation will result in economic losses for society. Governments, then, should do as little as possible — whether in taxation, regulation, or service provision. In an interview with National Public Radio (NPR) in the US, the American anti-tax lobbyist Grover Norquist famously summed up the idea this way: "I simply want to reduce it [government] to the size where I could drag it into the bathroom and drown it in the bathtub."[2]

A group of economists, led by American Milton Friedman, were behind the revival of laissez-faire economics when it was widely adopted during the 1980s Reagan-Thatcher-Mulroney era, and to this day Friedman's disciples continue to be strong proponents. They believe that market competition will force corporations to innovate and that progress will lead to benefits for everybody. In this model, competition brings multiple benefits: it allows highly skilled workers to demand higher wages, spurs technological advancement and results in lower prices for consumers.

The group promotes a simplistic version of the work of famed Scottish economist Adam Smith. In *The Wealth of Nations* in 1776, Smith used the metaphor of an "invisible hand" that ensures the advancement of social interest as the natural outcome of corporations and individuals acting in pursuit of their own self-interest. According to this theory, everything will balance if we leave it alone — akin to forces in physics.[3]

As most of us know from our own experience, however, it's not that simple. Joseph Stiglitz puts it this way: "Laws of economics are different from those of physics: markets are shaped by public policy, and most markets are far from competitive. Public policy shapes, in particular, who has how much market power."[4]

Competition only produces the results proponents claim if no participant in the market has enough power to set prices. The power to influence prices can come through market share, or through unequal information between buyers and sellers. The closer a market is to a monopoly (only one seller), or a monopsony (only one buyer), the more distorted market outcomes will be and the greater the opportunity for profit — usually through a combination of underpaying workers and overcharging consumers or through exploiting others who lack power.

Corporations and wealthy individuals are not looking for competition — they are looking for market power, such as pricing power or decision-making power. Corporations, and their executives, don't like competition because it drives profits and bonuses down. They will use whatever tactics they have at their disposal to eliminate their competition and increase their market share. This allows them the flexibility to reduce wages (workers have nowhere else to go), reduce the quality of their products, or increase prices to increase profits.[5] This dynamic in the global context has led to increasing market concentration in the last thirty years, and firms have used the market power that comes with it to make excessive profits by exploiting workers, consumers, Indigenous rights holders and the environment. With no intervention from governments, not only is there no wealth distribution, but we often end up in "winner-take-all" markets.

This scenario does not just create inequality — it amplifies existing inequalities. Those with more education, connections and wealth are often in a better position to eliminate the competition and gain even more wealth and power. For example, wealthier entrepreneurs can afford to buy out the competition or sell their own goods at a loss to price competitors out of the market. Well-connected individuals often have access to information that gives them an advantage. The barriers to entry for those without this kind of head start are daunting.

It is quite ironic that proponents of the free market theory call for no government intervention. But when it comes time to bail out big institutions like banks or when they need government intervention to rig the system in favour of the wealthiest individuals and big corporations, they don't hesitate to ask for government action. Pharmaceutical companies, for example, have no shame asking to increase the duration of their patents at every free-trade negotiation, so that they can eliminate competition for as long as possible and charge consumers more.

This leads us to a spin-off of this myth — the claim that we have "free-markets" in our current economy and that our greatest innovations have come from these free markets. As leading British economist on innovation policy and University of London professor Mariana Mazzucato has painstakingly detailed, many so-called private innovations depend heavily on public investment and research.[6] For example, the highly profitable iPhone wouldn't have been possible without publicly-funded breakthroughs at Bell Labs.

How do we explain the contradiction between the myth of free markets and the reality of the government's extensive role in establishing and regulating markets? The answer is simple: what the corporate advocates of this myth call a free market is really just a market designed to benefit the rich and the corporations and give them the freedom to behave as they wish. They want rules and public infrastructure and government intervention when it benefits them and exemptions from regulations and rules when it does not. Corporations are not looking for competition or even long-term economic growth. They are looking for short-term profits.

During the so-called free-market era starting in the early 1980s, governments reduced regulations, slashed corporate taxes and taxes on wealth, weakened labour protections, reduced social transfers and generally shaped markets to benefit the few. In what became essentially a global experiment, we tested the idea of reducing the government's role — in providing public services, distributing income and regulating the market. The results of this experiment are now in, and they are clear. As we have already documented in this book, the result has been greater economic inequality.

The evidence shows that a "free market" will always distribute more wealth to the top because people at the top always end up with more power and influence. This is where government should come into play, as an institution that balances things out. As economist Paul Krugman writes, we need to stop thinking that everyone is rational and that markets work perfectly. "Financial markets fall far short of perfection . . . they are subject to extraordinary delusions and the madness of crowds."[7] We need a neutral actor to intervene and put a stop to extreme inequalities and redistribute wealth fairly across society.

Myth No. 2 — Increase the Size of the Pie, and Everyone Will Benefit

The second myth that is often used to argue against measures that would redistribute wealth from the top to the broader citizenry is that increasing the size of the pie itself is the way to ensure everybody will get a bigger piece. In other words, if the economy grows — the GDP — everyone will benefit. We are often told by some academic and think-tank economists that government should focus on growth and not on wealth redistribution, because growth will benefit everyone whereas redistribution simply takes some of the existing pie from the better off to give to others.

Again, the evidence proves this myth false. As Canadian economist and expert on inequality Lars Osberg tells us, during what he calls the "managed-capitalism" era, Canada

> *had long depended on economic growth to paper over the social stresses created by economic inequality...For over 35 years now the gains from growth of national income have been disproportionately received by those at the top of Canada's income distribution.*[8]

The facts are clear: as the economy has grown in Canada, the benefits have almost all gone to a few people at the top. Simply put, most Canadians have received limited benefit from the country's increased wealth.

This has been true around the world. The *World Inequality Report 2018* showed that between 1980 and 2016 the poorest 50 per cent of humanity captured only 12 per cent of global income growth, while the top one per cent captured 27 per cent of it.[9] Canadian economist Armine Yalnizyan has coined the term "slowth" for the extended period of limited economic growth that many countries have been experiencing. She stresses the importance of shifting to an inclusive economic model to counter growing inequality.[10]

The reason why the pie portions will never grow equally without government intervention is simple — the portion going to people at the top is made on the backs of others. Big corporations may grow their "productivity" by finding ways to pay workers less for the same output, or by turning to automation. Either way, their gains come out of workers' pockets. A corporation's growth does not necessarily mean more jobs or higher wages for workers; usually, rich CEOs and shareholders reap most of the benefits of that growth.

Canadian Centre for Policy Alternatives economist David Macdonald documented this in his reports: he found that in 2019, the ratio of average CEO pay to average worker pay was 202:1. This ratio has dramatically increased since 1998 when the figure was 104:1.[11] As noted in Chapter 1, the average pay of a top one hundred CEO in 2019 was $10.8 million, compared to the average individual income of $53,482.[12]

Growth does not even necessarily mean better prices for consumers. As Joseph Stiglitz points out,

> *Higher profits can also arise from a better way of price discrimination, extracting "consumer surplus" (the excess of what individuals would be willing to pay for a product from what they would have to pay in a competitive market). The main effect of such exploitation is to redistribute income from consumers to our new super-wealthy and the firms they own and control.*[13]

Airlines, for example, demonstrate their corporate skill in extracting "consumer surplus" through constant changes in the price of seats. For example, they will increase prices in the last few days before departure, having learned that people who book last-minute flights generally have to travel and will therefore pay more than people who book far in advance and have more options about when and where to travel. Before developing these skills, airlines set a single price on a trip that applied no matter when the ticket was purchased.

Proponents of this neoliberal approach have it backwards. If we don't address inequality first, growth suffers. As economist Andrew Jackson notes,

> *Many prominent economists . . . argue that mounting inequality has been a significant factor behind "secular stagnation," an extended period of very slow growth as surplus profits and savings sit largely idle while households seek to reduce their debts.*[14]

Economist Lars Osberg reports,

> *There is now a growing chorus of economists arguing that increasing inequality implies Western economies have a structural tendency to secular stagnation, due to an excess and ever-increasing flow of savings coming from the rising incomes of the very affluent.*[15]

The pie would grow more quickly if the incomes of ordinary Canadians were rising along with the economy's greater productivity.

Another reason the myth does not fit with the facts? A pie is a pretty bad metaphor for how the economy actually works. In the 1980s, the iconoclastic British-American economist Hazel Henderson came up with a better model to explain how the economy works — a layer cake. In Henderson's model, the market economy is supported by our natural environment, unpaid care work and public infrastructure.

More recently, University of Oxford economist Kate Raworth has used the analogy of a doughnut — with the outside of the doughnut representing finite natural resources (our ceiling) and the inside representing our social foundation (the desired floor, comprising all the basic necessities, such as food, clothing, shelter, health care and education).[16] Any model that removes people's basic needs and our natural environment's limits from an understanding of the economy is bound to come out with the wrong answers.

Myth No. 3 — The "Trickle-Down" of Wealth from the Top Benefits Everyone

The third myth we often encounter? If we cut taxes for the richest or for big corporations and make them better off, the benefits will "trickle down" to the rest of us. Investors and corporations will reinvest their tax savings, create jobs and grow our economy. This myth provided the rationale for most of the tax cuts we discussed in Chapter 1. As Paul Krugman says, the doctrine that low taxes on the wealthy are the secret of prosperity has been tested again and again since the 1980s… Few economic doctrines have been as thoroughly tested and thoroughly refuted, as the claim that low taxes on the rich accomplish great things for everyone. Yet the doctrine persists.[17]

Indeed, following every economic crisis, this myth has invariably resurfaced, with some proposing, among other things, that we cut taxes for the wealthiest to stimulate the economy. The problem, as we shall see, is that tax cuts do *not* trickle down. Instead, they increase economic inequality considerably and do not create significant economic activity. Therefore, cutting taxes for the richest really only helps the richest — and it hurts the rest of us.

A study by London School of Economics economists David Hope and Julian Limberg, published in December 2020, analyzed more than fifty years of tax cuts for the richest in eighteen major European and North American OECD countries, and found very conclusively that the trickle-down theory is false. Their conclusion states:

> *Major reforms reducing taxes on the rich lead to higher income inequality as measured by the top 1% share of pre-tax national income. The effect remains stable in the medium term. In contrast, such reforms do not have any significant effect on economic growth and unemployment.*[18]

With data across fifty years and eighteen countries, this research offers definitive evidence that "trickle-down" is nothing more than a comforting myth offered to the public. The myth hides the simple fact that reducing taxes on rich people and big corporations makes them wealthier and increases the gap between the one per cent and everyone else. Contrary to the claims, lower taxes on the rich do not generate jobs and do not "trickle down" to the rest of the population in any way.

In fact, lower taxes on the rich hurt the rest of us because governments often pay for those tax cuts by reducing the quantity or quality of public services they offer. In an interview about his findings in late 2020, David Hope noted one implication of the research: "Policy makers shouldn't worry that raising taxes on the rich to fund the financial costs of the pandemic will harm their economies."[19]

It's easy to see the truth that the myth hides. As Paul Krugman explains, "Give a family with an annual income of $20,000 an extra $1,000, and it will make a big difference to their lives. Give a guy who makes $1 million an extra thousand, and he'll barely notice it."[20] More importantly, the family with an income near the national average or lower will spend that $1,000 in their local communities, while the richest likely will not.

In Canada, the Canada Child Benefit (CCB) has offered a good example of what support for families can mean for the economy. By making life more affordable in a progressive way, this benefit not only brought the income of many families in Canada over the poverty threshold but it also significantly stimulated the economy.[21] The reason is simple: those families spent the money to buy things that they needed — like food and winter clothes that they would have otherwise gone without.

By contrast, when we give more money to the richest, they don't need it, so they don't necessarily spend it. Joseph Stiglitz also explains that "as money moves from the bottom of the economic pyramid to the top, aggregate consumption is lowered simply because those at the top consume a smaller fraction of their income than those below, who have to spend virtually all of their income just to get by."[22]

What is true at the individual level is also true for corporations. For example, in the twenty-first century the federal corporate tax rate was cut from 28 per cent to 15 per cent in Canada. Economist David Macdonald reviewed the impact of this policy change and concluded:

> *Canada's long running (and very expensive) experiment in corporate tax rates — to see if lowering them to compete with U.S. levels leads to extra investment in the economy — was more or less a failure. Companies used the differential to enrich themselves and their shareholders.*[23]

The level of corporate investment in 2020 was about the same as in 2000, before the cuts were implemented.[24] Not only did they not invest the "savings," but they used this money to make payments to their shareholders through dividends or share buybacks. Between 2000 and 2018, these payments doubled as a share of GDP. In dollar terms, they have gone from $76 billion to $281 billion a year.[25]

When corporations have not used their tax savings as payouts to rich CEOs, shareholders, or owners, it seems they have left that money sitting in their bank accounts, as if they had no clue about how to invest it profitably. As Macdonald points out, Canadians would all be better off if the federal government had kept that money to invest in ways that would benefit everyone — like a universal national pharmacare system.[26]

Alberta Premier Jason Kenney's corporate tax cut offers yet another example. After the rate was lowered from 12 to 11 per cent, it was estimated that the biggest oil and gas companies in Alberta — such as Suncor, Cenovus and Husky — boosted their net income by $2 billion.[27] Meanwhile, Suncor announced in October 2020 that it planned to eliminate between 10 and 15 per cent of its workforce over the succeeding eighteen months — representing roughly 2,000 lost jobs — while the company got a big tax cut from the government. Husky pocketed the windfall while laying off hundreds in Calgary. Worse still, at the same time, Kenney cut about 11,000 jobs in the health care system and 20,000 education support staff jobs. In sum, Albertans paid for corporate tax cuts with fewer jobs and services.

Canadians always end up paying the price of corporate tax cuts, because by definition they mean less revenue for the government. As shown by an analysis by the *Toronto Star* and *Corporate Knights* magazine in 2017, Canadians not only had to cover the tab by getting less and less in public services and supports, but they also had to pay more taxes themselves to cover the shortfall.

Sixty-five years ago, people and corporations contributed equal amounts of income tax to the Canadian government, but as of 2017 people paid three and a half times more than corporations.[28] Tax cuts for corporations don't yield trickle-down benefits to the public. They mostly go toward further enriching the wealthiest and, therefore, increasing our societal inequalities.

World-renowned economists and tax experts, including Emmanuel Saez, Gabriel Zucman and Peter Diamond, have shown that, if implemented well, higher tax rates could be highly beneficial for the economy. We will address this later, but their research underlines the fact that proponents of trickle-down economics have it backwards. If we want to improve the quality of life for everyone in Canada, including the richest among us, we need to ensure that the wealthiest individuals and big corporations pay their fair share, instead of giving them more money.

Myth No. 4 — Taxing the Wealthy Constitutes Theft

The myth that raising taxes on the wealthy is a kind of theft rests on the premise that these people deserve to keep their money because they worked for it, earned it and should not be taxed more just because they have been successful. As Paul Krugman points out, economists and people who believe this, "view government intervention to reduce inequality and risk as immoral. Taxing the rich to help the poor, as they see it, is a form of theft, no matter how laudable the purpose."[29] Stories of high-tech billionaires who started from scratch and succeeded are used to prove that the system is fair and anyone can make it if they work hard enough. The super-rich themselves often argue we should not ask them to pay more, because they created our jobs and wealth (see trickle-down myth, above); they often threaten — implicitly or explicitly — to leave the country if they have to pay more.

Here is some evidence relevant to this theory: The fortunes of many of the richest people in Canada come from family inheritance. More than half of the wealthiest eighty-seven families in Canada inherited a large part of their wealth, including all but one of the top ten on the *Canadian Business* 2017 list of the richest Canadians.[30] Many of these fortunes have grown because of strategic financial investments, not necessarily because of hard work. Also, as we have already shown in this chapter, a portion of these fortunes resulted from tax cuts for the wealthiest.

As the OECD has observed, "wealth begets wealth."[31] People with more money can easily make more money because they have access to things that others don't. For example, wealthy people:

- Can borrow money at a lower rate, allowing them to borrow more and use that to accumulate more wealth.
- Already own things that they can charge rents on.
- Have access to tax loopholes that others don't.
- Can take risks during financial crises when others can't.[32]

Also, fortunes made in the financial sector, often based on purely speculative and unproductive activities, show that wealth creation and productive economic contribution do not necessarily go hand in hand.[33]

The fortunes of many of the wealthiest Canadian families are based on ownership of one or more large corporations. The businesses owned by billionaires such as the Desmarais family, Jim Pattison, the Irvings, the Thomsons, the Westons, the McCains and others contribute to the Canadian economy with jobs while they earn profits and grow the wealth of their owners. As we have discussed, these corporations are often dominant in their markets, giving them leverage to achieve higher growth and returns by limiting competition, driving wages down, controlling costs, increasing prices and lobbying governments to heed their interests and expand their economic power — all to make their owner(s) even wealthier.

As we have seen, inside those big corporations, CEOs and managers will often receive compensation well beyond their real productive contribution. This system of executive pay rewards those who boost short-term profits that can be distributed to the shareholders (who often have no role in running the company). This wealth results from a system that allows and even facilitates these holders of great wealth to continue growing rich, without limit.

Even if we imagine the possibility that some billionaires created their wealth through their own clever innovations and hard work, they would still owe a great deal of their success to the broader society. Thomas Piketty, author of the definitive book on the tendency of capital to capture a growing share of wealth in the world, offers this explanation:

> *The accumulation of wealth is always the fruit of a social process, which depends, among other things, on public infrastructures (such as legal, fiscal and educational systems), the social division of labour and the knowledge accumulated by humanity over centuries. Under such conditions, it is perfectly logical that people who have accumulated large amounts of wealth should return a fraction of it to the community each year.*[34]

Businesses benefit from important public infrastructure such as roads, railways, ports and airports, but they also benefit from government-sponsored social programs. Child care is a good example. In provinces where a child care system has been implemented, such as Quebec and British Columbia, businesses benefit greatly from the positive impacts of such a program.

The same would be true for national universal pharmacare. Such programs are sometimes a factor that corporations and wealthy individuals consider when deciding whether to set up shop in our country. In other words, the government does not steal money from the richest when it collects higher taxes; it collects a return based on the contribution of public infrastructure to private profits.

The theory that taxing the wealthy constitutes theft triggers the following question: how can the extreme wealth that we see today be justified? What is the point of individuals having so much money when most of them would never be able to spend it over the course of multiple lifetimes, even if they wanted to?

A billionaire would have to spend $10 million every year of life from age 0 to 100 to run out of his first billion dollars. As Paul Krugman noted,

> *Anyone accumulating riches on this scale could easily afford to raise the pay of the employees who generate their wealth, or contribute a great deal more in taxes to support vital public services, while remaining very well rewarded for whatever successes they've achieved.*[35]

A policy that would make the rich pay their fair share will barely affect their life satisfaction, because they will still be able to buy whatever they wish.

Conclusion

In this chapter, we have summarized the four main theories used to defend the wealth and income of the richest people in Canada and elsewhere in the world, and to fend off proposals to tax the one per cent to reduce inequality and allow governments to pay for more and better services to the public that will improve their lives.

We have cited the evidence that demonstrates how these theories are contradicted by the facts. Frustratingly, they are zombie myths — the type that live on and are persistently cited despite clear evidence that they are false. The myths buttress inequality denial, which rivals climate denial as an effort to deflect action on issues that require urgent attention. In both cases, big corporations and wealthy individuals work hard to stave off any meaningful action and to maintain their wealth and power.

Those holding great wealth and power have no interest in changing the system; indeed they will fight such efforts. If we want to change things, there is much work to be done. It won't be easy, but it can be done.

CHAPTER 3

THE CHOICES THAT CREATED ECONOMIC INEQUALITY

Extreme inequality is not inevitable. It has been a political choice, and it remains one. We may have strong feelings about some choices or actions from wealthy people, but individuals are not the problem. This is a systemic problem — a problem that results from how our political and economic systems are designed and how they work.

The extreme inequalities in Canada were not caused by a few bad apples. They are the result of successive political decisions from Liberal and Conservative governments that rigged the system in favour of the richest. As we explored in the last chapter, those decisions were justified by the myth that by making the wealthiest richer, prosperity would "trickle down" to the rest of the population.

Economist Andrew Jackson sums up the situation:

> *Rising inequality is the result of the deliberate reversal of the post-war social contract, combined with the more anonymous economic forces of globalization*

> *and technological change. This has set the stage for pernicious social consequences and poses the clear danger of a prolonged period of economic stagnation.*[1]

The approach taken after the Second World War — which allowed a large middle class in many countries, including Canada, to benefit from the economy's growth and wealth — has been abandoned. For the past thirty years, almost all the increased wealth generated in Canada has gone to the top ten per cent. In fact, most has gone to the top one per cent.

When Ronald Reagan, Margaret Thatcher, and Brian Mulroney held power in the 1980s, their governments put an end to the share-the-wealth policies of the postwar period. Under the new approach, prosperity was supposed to come from the corporate sector. These leaders declared government the enemy of the people, and instituted a wide range of measures to cut back on government services and regulation:

- Taxes — especially those paid by the wealthy — were cut, making it hard for governments to continue providing services to the public.
- Government regulations on industry were described as "red tape" and cut back.
- Important businesses owned by governments — airlines, railways, power systems, transit systems, highways, water companies, and many more — were sold to corporations, often at bargain basement prices.

Politicians, lobbyists, and business spokespeople used the myths we reviewed in Chapter 2 to argue that these changes were necessary for a healthy economy. It is now obvious that this approach was bad for ordinary people, but incredibly good for the one per cent.

During the Reagan-Thatcher-Mulroney era, many governments around the world followed their philosophy of cutting services to which people had access and withdrawing state intervention in many spheres. Full employment was largely abandoned as a key objective of government macroeconomic policy as part of this overhaul. The financial sector was deregulated, creating vast new opportunities for profits and increasing pressure on the rest of the economy to maximize short-term profits.[2]

Globalization and Flexible Labour Markets

Across the world, many regard labour with an attitude that amounts to hostility. At one time, a highly skilled and reliable workforce was considered an asset for a country's economy and prosperity. Today, much as it was a century ago, labour is almost universally viewed as a cost that must be minimized.

Governments have focused on enabling flexibility for employers, making decisions that deliberately weakened trade unions and reduced employment standards. They have enabled corporations to move their operations to countries where workers are paid less. This has of course resulted in fewer high-wage jobs in prosperous countries like Canada, and it has also undermined the bargaining power of Canadian workers. Overall, these developments have reduced the share of corporations' income that goes to workers rather than to owners, and also reduced the relative wages of so-called unskilled and semiskilled workers.

The rise of globalization allowed large companies to adopt a number of practices that have been harmful to workers:

- Relocating jobs to countries where labour is exploited eliminated jobs at home and put even more pressure on workers.
- Outsourcing and subcontracting, within Canada or globally, has proved an effective way to break unions and reduce workers' bargaining power.
- Shifting toward part-time workforces and workers from temp agencies has allowed employers to easily punish

workers who questioned exploitative practices or tried to stand up for their rights at work.

- Allowing employers to hire migrant workers on temporary work visas that are not transferable to any other employer in Canada has left these workers extremely exposed to being exploited. Workers who speak up are sent home and not allowed to come back, a huge financial cost for themselves and their families.

Furthermore, Canada, like many other governments, signed a whole slew of free trade agreements that give considerable new powers to corporations over states and workers. Competition for low-paid and relatively low-skilled jobs that are not subject to replacement by machinery or offshoring has increased, leading to a highly polarized labour market.[3] With the advance in robotics, artificial intelligence, and other innovations, more and more people have lost their jobs (or fear losing them), disrupting the labour market even more.

All of this significantly reduced the cost of labour for employers in Canada. Unit labour costs equal the total compensation that a company pays to a worker to get one unit of output. These costs grew at an average rate of just 0.5 per cent per year between 1993 and 1999, and 2.1 per cent in the first decade of the twenty-first century, down from an average of 6.6 per cent over the previous two decades.[4]

The impact? To concentrate income into the hands of business owners — in particular the owners of giant corporations with large workforces. This shift was justified by the explanation that the wealth would "trickle down." But as we saw Bay Street's fortunes going up, workers' fortunes were going down. As Andrew Jackson summarized,

> *Extreme inequality has primarily been driven by trends in the labour market and by the increasing share of capital in income. It is primarily a question of*

> *"pre-distribution" from the market, albeit driven by inadequate government measures to counteract the forces driving greater inequality.*[5]

In other words, the total share of national income in Canada that goes to workers earning salaries and wages shrank, while the share going to the owners of capital grew. And the biggest winners were the people who own the most capital — in other words, the one per cent — and even more so the tiny group of Canadian billionaires and multimillionaires, plus the foreign multinationals and their owners, which play such a large role in our economic life.

The changing dynamics in the Canadian labour market had stark impacts on workers facing COVID-19. Higher-wage workers were more likely to be able to work from home or had sufficient bargaining power to demand safety protocols in their workplaces. Lower-wage workers were more likely to be laid off or to continue working without appropriate safety measures or paid sick leave.

This explains COVID-19 outbreaks in agriculture, food processing, and many long-term care homes. Black and racialized workers are disproportionately represented in these jobs and are more likely to live in large households with family members who work in these industries as well. The failure to protect low-wage workers in these environments meant they and their families experienced a much higher incidence of COVID-19. Politicians and pundits sometimes blamed this outcome on cultural differences, but the real story was the role systemic labour market discrimination played in causing this result.

A Shrinking Federal Government and a Frayed Social Safety Net

A decade or so after the shift to the Reagan-Thatcher-Mulroney policies, in the 1990s, Canada and other countries shifted investment away from the middle and working class by cutting social programs such as unemployment insurance and social assistance. This also tipped the scales in favour of big corporations and against unions and workers. Paul Martin — then finance minister — reduced employers' contribution to unemployment insurance, slashed benefits to unemployed workers, and used the $54 billion surplus these decisions created to "balance the books" of the federal government. This money had come from and belonged to workers, yet it vanished with no accountability — and the Liberals basked in this fiscal "accomplishment."

As part of this focus on balancing the books and eliminating the federal budget deficit, Paul Martin reduced spending on federal government programs and transfers to provinces, cities, and individuals by 5 per cent of GDP from 1993 to 2000, an enormous amount.[6] In an article in *The Tyee* in 2015, economist and researcher Michal Rozworski noted,

> *Reduced fiscal transfers to provinces put the squeeze on local governments. Since the 1990s, Canada has seen provincial governments . . . impose austerity further down the line. Since provinces are responsible for many basics like health, education, and welfare benefits, shrinking transfers have further eroded the working class's social wage. Privatizations, workfare schemes, tuition increases — all were applied (unevenly) across the country.*[7]

Because of those cuts, poverty rates remained stubbornly high for most of the 1990s, and the incomes of the bottom half of households rose only very modestly, despite falling unemployment. In addition to all those cuts, Paul Martin failed to act on two significant Liberal promises[8] — a national child care and early learning program (1993) and a national pharmacare program (1997).

Once the debt crisis passed, the federal government decided

to cut taxes for the wealthy rather than undo cuts to funding for health, education, and other social programs. The Liberal governments of Jean Chrétien and Paul Martin cut corporate tax rates from 27 to 21 per cent between 2000 and 2004, and cut the capital gains inclusion rate (the proportion of income from capital gains that is considered taxable income) from 75 to 50 per cent.

The cut in taxing capital gains has been particularly good for the one per cent. Capital gains are the amounts an investor makes from selling an investment asset, such as real estate (other than a primary residence) or stocks. This income is treated differently from income from wages and employment. The inclusion rate is used to reduce a dollar of income earned from capital gains when it is added to an investor's income — instead of treating the dollar from capital gains as a dollar, the inclusion rate reduces the dollar to a smaller amount.

The rule had been that a dollar of capital gains was treated as just seventy-five cents of income, for tax purposes. Jean Chrétien and Paul Martin reduced that rate to fifty cents. Nine-tenths of the benefit of this measure has gone to the top one per cent in Canada.[9] (We should remember that in private life Paul Martin was the wealthy owner of Canada Steamship Lines until 2003, when he turned the company over to his sons. His family is an established member of the one per cent.)

The trend of reducing taxes for the one per cent continued once Stephen Harper was elected prime minister in 2006. His government introduced steep cuts for the richest by further reducing corporate tax rates from 21 to 15 per cent.

Over this relatively short time period, Canada went from being one of the most redistributive countries in the OECD to one of the least redistributive countries. Inequality grew because of a trend toward a less progressive tax system, including a reduction in top tax rates and a reduction in investment income taxes.

As Andrew Jackson, together with fellow economist Toby Sanger, explained,

> *Many factors have contributed to growing inequalities, but significantly they include tax policy changes that lowered tax rates for capital and business income, particularly during the 2000–2015 period. A 2016 study modelling historical changes in wealth distribution in the United States found that "the most important factor — by far — behind the developments [in wealth inequality] is the significant decline in tax progressivity that began in the late 1970s.*[10]

Analysis of the incidence of the overall Canadian tax system (including income, sales, payroll, property, and other taxes) found that tax policy measures reduced the overall effective tax rate on the top one per cent to the extent that by 2005 it was lower than the rate for all other income groups, including the lowest income decile.

In other words, Canada's one per cent benefited from tax changes over fifteen years that left them paying a lower rate of taxes than virtually every other taxpayer in the country.

The special investigation by the *Toronto Star* and *Corporate Knights* in 2017 reported:

> *Sixty-five years ago, people and corporations contributed equal amounts of income tax to the Canadian government. Since then, the scales have tipped in the corporations' favour. Corporate taxes have been slashed, and people have been forced to make up the difference. [In 2015–2016, Canadians] paid $145 billion in income tax, while corporations paid $41 billion.*[11]

Canada's 102 largest corporations — those worth more than $2 billion — were supposed to pay the statutory corporate tax rate of 26.6 per cent. The same investigation found that they actually paid 17.7 per cent in tax in the years 2011–16. This gap of 8.9 per cent between the statutory rate and their effective rate is equivalent to a $62.9 billion transfer from public books to corporations' pockets.[12]

It's important to note that corporations could have lowered their effective tax rates by re-investing their profits into research and development, intellectual property, or machinery and equipment. The data show us that even with specific tax cuts meant to encourage investment in research and development (R&D) or machinery and equipment, Canadian businesses have shifted to holding more and more of their assets in cash. This is what then Bank of Canada governor Mark Carney referred to as "dead money" in 2012, but his admonishment seems to have been ignored as the trend has continued. Perhaps somewhat

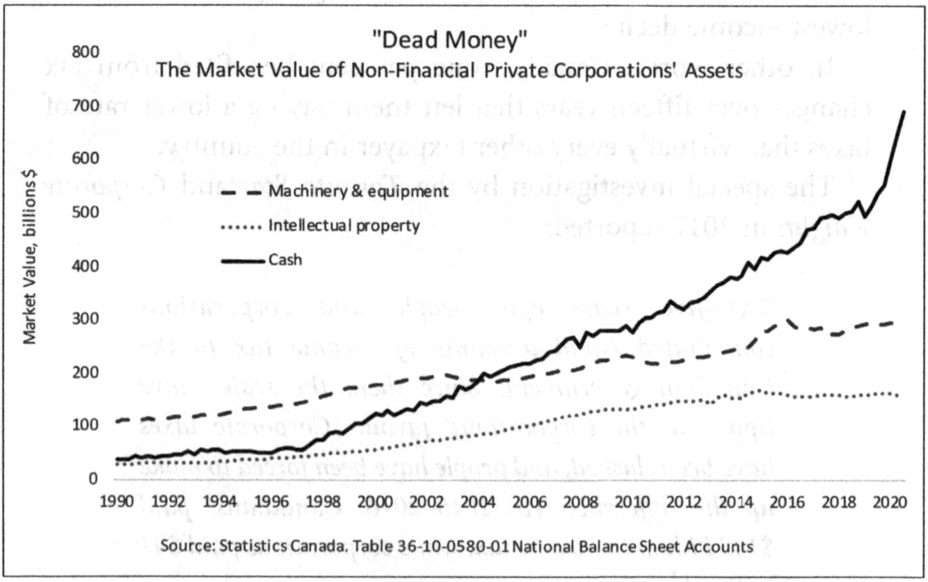

ironically, reductions in the statutory tax rate for corporations may have encouraged this trend, because they reduced the amount of tax savings companies could get for these more productive investments.

Canadian banks are the "best" of all Canadian companies at reducing their tax bills, and they have been getting better at it over time. Between 2010 and 2015, the profits of Canada's big banks grew by 60 per cent, but the rate of tax they paid on their earnings actually dropped. They manage to do this year after year because of tax loopholes that no government has dared to tackle, such as the use of subsidiaries in tax havens that shift profits out of Canada.

The effect of these tax cuts was dramatic. Between Chrétien, Martin, and Harper, federal revenues were slashed by over $50 billion per year, with most of that money returning to the wealthiest among us, instead of being used to pay for the universal services we all need and want. With less federal funding, the provinces have had to pick up a greater share of funding for essential services like education and health care. And provincial governments have followed the federal lead in cutting corporate taxes, leaving them with even less revenue to cover the federal shortfall and providing further benefits to the top one per cent.

These years of austerity, cutbacks, and deregulation created cracks in the system that were dramatically revealed during the COVID-19 pandemic. Crowded classrooms made it more difficult to make schools safe. Reliance on private, for-profit long-term care put workers and many of our loved ones' lives at risk. Municipalities that relied on user fees to fund public transit were left with sudden enormous shortfalls in their budgets. Universities have relied on skyrocketing tuition costs to cover reduced public funding, leaving students with mounting debt at exactly the moment they faced an unpromising labour market.

In recent decades, the advent of technology has created new

opportunities, but also new challenges, including appropriately taxing web giants such as Amazon, Apple, Google, Facebook, and Netflix. Those big multinationals control almost everything in their respective industries and are used to being able to set the agenda. They use their wealth and power to make sure that regulators see things their way.

Up to 2021, this meant they paid no tax of any kind on their activities in Canada. Moreover, they were not subject to the same rules as other businesses in Canada — thus creating a tilted and unfair playing field. The tech giants used this huge advantage to make enormous profits and push out smaller competitors. Their presence has forced many small businesses and local newspapers to close their doors and made it harder for many artists and musicians to make a living doing what they love to do.

In 2020, the federal government announced its plan to ensure that those tech companies collect the GST/HST on the physical and digital goods they sell. This makes sense as we work toward a level playing field between Canadian businesses and the tech giants. But it is Canadian consumers who would pay GST/HST, not those big tech companies.

Here we see the federal government taking the path of least resistance and failing to directly confront corporate powers to address the root problem. France moved forward in 2020 to require those companies to pay their fair share, and Canada should too. Otherwise, inequalities of revenue and power between these select multinationals and Canadian businesses will only continue to grow.

Corporate Transparency and Tax Havens

In addition to all the changes that have come about since the advent of Reagan-Thatcher-Mulroney policies in the early 1980s, the wealthiest individuals and biggest corporations started to use tax havens more and more during the same period. Tax havens —

paradis fiscaux in French — are countries big and small that allow companies to do business while paying little or no tax to the local government. Often the companies are even allowed to hide their true ownership.

What makes a country that operates as a tax haven attractive for foreign companies? Many countries, including Canada, allow their companies and their citizens to set up fake corporations in tax havens that are structured to record profits that were really earned in Canada. When the profits are recorded in the tax havens instead of in Canada, Canadian laws do not require Canadian companies to pay taxes on those profits. Using tax havens, big corporations can reduce their real tax rates dramatically — often down to zero.

Economist and tax expert Toby Sanger explains that tax havens result directly from the work of large international financial institutions that operate in big cities like London, Toronto, and New York. Those financial institutions function like private clubs where only the wealthiest members have access to special tricks for avoiding taxes and other obligations in their respective countries.

Using the same flawed philosophy that help for the richest would "trickle down" to the rest of society, governments actually made it easier for individuals and corporations to avoid paying taxes — by signing tax agreements and treaties with tax haven countries. Governments, including the Canadian government, made it easier for the wealthy to set up shell corporations, trusts, and foundations, for the specific purpose of sheltering their profits from taxes in their home countries.[13]

Canadian governments are particularly lax when it comes to regulating corporate transparency, making it easier for companies and wealthy individuals to hide their assets, minimize their income, and avoid paying taxes. The well-known financial journalist Diane Francis calls Canada a "secrecy haven,"[14] because our laws make it easy for shell corporations to hide their ownership, as well as money sources and destinations. This has implications for corruption and international money laundering, as well as tax avoidance and evasion through tax havens.

As with the labour market, free trade agreements and globalization exacerbated these problems. Multinational corporations have now been able to choose from among many tax haven jurisdictions to reduce their tax bills. The consequences of tax havens have been made even worse by a race-to-the-bottom competition between politicians and tax haven jurisdictions. International organizations like the OECD, World Bank, and IMF accelerated the rhetoric about which countries cut corporate tax the most, or which offered the weakest labour and environmental regulations for foreign businesses to attract "job creators." On top of that, financial innovation, the information technology revolution, and the digitalization of the economy have taken tax avoidance to yet another dimension.[15]

Sanger further explains:

> *While wealthy individuals may just use one or two tax havens, corporations will establish subsidiaries in a number of different ones, with each serving a separate purpose. The multiplicity of tax havens further helps companies hide their assets and hedge their bets, in case political and public sentiment in one country turns the other way. And because the preferences provided by tax havens are generally always only available for foreign firms, having multinationals straddle many jurisdictions makes it easier for them to avoid taxes in all of them. For instance, at a time when it was the most valuable company in the world, Apple was able to transfer much of its wealth to subsidiaries that were not considered resident for tax purposes anywhere in*

the world, and to pay an effective tax rate of just 0.005 per cent.[16]

To be clear, a tax rate of 0.005 per cent means that for every million dollars of profit it recorded, Apple paid just $50 in taxes.

The use of tax havens by wealthy individuals and big corporations, as well as the fact that successive Liberal and Conservative governments have refused to tackle this plague, have made inequalities in our country far worse. Between 1988 and 2018, assets reported by Canadian corporations located in the top twelve tax havens skyrocketed from $9 billion to $353 billion, more than doubling as a share of total Canadian direct investment abroad, from 11 per cent to 27 per cent.[17] As the Parliamentary Budget Officer estimated, Canadian corporations moved nearly a trillion dollars to offshore destinations through legal tax avoidance schemes in 2016 alone. The wealth hidden away from the tax authorities in that single year represents a loss to the Canadian government of as much as $25 billion annually.[18]

Conclusion

As we have seen, wealth begets power, and power begets more wealth. The inequalities in our society did not appear overnight or by accident. They have been created and sustained over many years and by many conscious decisions from our governments to tip the scale in favour of the richest. Our system has been rigged. It lets wealthy individuals and mega corporations amass jaw-dropping wealth. This is wealth that could not have been created without our public infrastructure, our public research, and most importantly, our labour. Time and again when our federal government promises to change the system, the responsible government ministers and senior officials find a way to turn their backs on the many and stand up for the few.

Both Liberals and Conservatives justify those decisions by

using assumptions, theories, and myths that have been proven wrong. So do the lobbyists, think tankers, and academics who serve the interests of the one per cent. All of them are promoting fiscal denial, which is every bit as dangerous and wrong as climate denial.

In early 2021, it seemed clear that once we were beyond the pandemic, the government would be looking to "put our house in order." Within the status quo, this generally means tax cuts for the rich and service cuts for the rest of us. It has also meant higher taxes for ordinary Canadians, even while the one per cent are given ways to pay less.

That is why it is so important for us to demand changes that will allow us to share Canada's wealth, instead of allowing the one per cent to benefit most from our country's riches and the work that ordinary Canadians do every day. Fair taxes are key to a better Canada. We can pursue that goal by organizing and applying the necessary pressure so we can build a fairer society.

PART TWO:
SHARE THE WEALTH — HOW WE CAN DO IT

As we saw in the previous section, economic inequalities and their consequences are not inevitable. They are the result of political decisions designed to purposefully favour the wealthy. The responsibility for social mobility, or lack of it, does not rest only on the shoulders of individuals. Hard work and the right education are not enough to land a good job with good working conditions, good insurance, and a salary that provides a degree of comfort. More and more Canadians, finding themselves or someone close to them stuck in a precarious and stressful economic situation, are realizing this. This is not something we should accept as part of a natural cycle or an unavoidable reality.

Real solutions to our problematic economic circumstances exist. They require us to roll up our sleeves, get organized, work hard, and have the courage to confront those who resist the creation of a fairer world. Those who benefit from the current rules and structures will tell us that it's too hard, it's not practical, it's not fair, and wealth really does trickle down. But as we have shown in Part One, the evidence overwhelmingly indicates that these are myths and that a different way of organizing our economy is possible. Different decisions and new approaches will allow us to diminish inequalities and significantly mitigate the many problems that arise from inequality in Canadian society.

In Part Two, we will discuss solutions put forward by the NDP and many economic and tax policy experts. These solutions are practical, well adapted to our current reality, and not based on zombie economic myths. We will present our proposals one at a time in separate chapters, but we want to stress that no single measure is enough to address inequality in Canada on its own. We will need a combination of several strong and effective policy measures to achieve our goals.

CHAPTER 4

TAXING INDIVIDUAL WEALTH

In recent years, the idea of a wealth tax has made a comeback in the political debate as a way to tackle extreme wealth and provide the government with a new source of revenue to pay for better services for society. The idea is not new. Wealth taxes have been in place for decades, and remain in use in some parts of the world. This proposal has resurfaced because our tax system and that of many other countries favours the richest and has failed to address economic inequalities.

Canadian economists Andrew Jackson and Toby Sanger were early advocates of a wealth tax for Canada. They wrote,

> *The major goal of a wealth tax is to counter the extreme concentration of wealth and to throw light on the concentration of wealth. It should complement other progressive taxes such as a steeply progressive personal income tax and high, effective corporate income tax rates.*[1]

In this chapter, we look at this measure in some detail: what constitutes a wealth tax, what it should look like in Canada, and why we should put one in place.

What Is a Wealth Tax?

A "wealth tax" is usually a broad-based tax on wealth that often includes all or most types of assets an individual or a household can own, such as real estate, cars, luxury items (art objects, jewellery, etc.), and investments. An individual or household's wealth — or net worth —is the sum of all those assets minus all debts (mortgage, credit card, student loans, etc.). As an example, if you own a $500,000 house and a $50,000 car and have $100,000 in stocks, but you also have a mortgage of $250,000 and a student loan of $30,000, your wealth would be calculated as $650,000 minus $280,000, for a net wealth of $370,000.

There are different forms of wealth taxes, and even in Canada many people already pay taxes on wealth. Here, as in many countries, property owners pay an annual tax on the value of their property. Property taxes rarely consider debts, and the amount of the tax is normally determined solely based on the asset's assessed value. An annual wealth tax is similar in principle but includes a larger set of assets — under such a system, not only property but a person or household's entire wealth is taxed.

The wealth tax that we propose is more specifically referred to as an "annual net wealth tax." The suggested rate for such taxes is usually pretty low — 1 or 2 per cent — and focused on individuals and families with wealth over a certain minimum threshold. The threshold varies from jurisdiction to jurisdiction and is determined based on several factors, but often targets what we would call the super-wealthy — people with wealth of many millions.

We will see many examples below, but the NDP's plan is to implement a 1 per cent annual tax on wealth above $20 million. In Canada, people who own more than $20 million are the tenth of one per cent (0.1 per cent). There are an estimated 13,800 households who would pay this tax, out of our total of 14 million.

A wealth tax is different from the tax we are most familiar with, income tax, which we see on our pay stubs and when we file our annual income tax return. This tax is based on the income we receive. For most of us that comes from working, although some of us get income from pensions or other investments. A wealth tax, by contrast, is based on the value of assets that people hold. This means a person may have to pay it even if they don't work.

Wealth and property taxes are among the oldest forms of taxes, but as part of the general trend we explored in Part One — of tax cuts for the richest starting in the 1980s — most of the world's annual wealth taxes have been eliminated.[2] As of 2021, only a few countries had a wealth tax. The decline in wealth taxes has taken place not because the taxes are ineffective, but because the vested interests that influence government policy decisions have been successful in arguing for their elimination, often using the four myths as reasons for the changes.

Close attention must be paid to how a wealth tax is designed. Certain elements can affect how easy it is to avoid, how hard it is to enforce, and how fair it appears to taxpayers. We can learn from failed attempts to implement wealth taxes and avoid the mistakes that other countries have made.

First, wealth taxes in European Union (EU) countries had lots of exemptions, excluding certain classes of assets such as art. These exemptions made the tax more expensive to enforce and created economic distortions. Having some exemptions also seems less fair, and spurs interest groups to lobby for even more exemptions.

Second, the threshold for EU wealth taxes was set too low. The tax was low enough that small family-owned businesses had enough assets for the tax to apply to them but often didn't have enough revenue to afford the tax.

Finally, it was fairly easy for millionaires in the EU to move to a lower-tax jurisdiction (which does not really apply in North America). For a rich French citizen, hopping over the border to a lower-tax jurisdiction like Luxembourg or Monaco proved an attractive alternative to staying in France. Moving between EU countries was made simple by the close integration in the economic and monetary union — where barriers to studying in or commuting to neighbouring countries would result in almost no impact on daily life for the millionaire's family.

In the Organisation for Economic Co-operation and Development (OECD), Switzerland, Norway, and Spain had wealth taxes as of 2021 — of these three countries, only Spain is a member of the EU.[3]

- Spain now taxes wealth above €700,000 at 0.2 per cent, which gradually increases to 2.5 per cent on net worth above €10.7 million depending on the region.
- The Norwegian government levies a tax at a rate of 0.15 per cent, and municipalities impose a 0.7 per cent rate, bringing the maximum tax rate to 0.85 per cent for wealth above $216,000 CAD (roughly 1.48 million krona).
- In Switzerland, the rate varies among the 26 cantons into which the country is divided, from 0.3 per cent to 1 per cent of taxpayers' net worth above $335,690 CAD (250,000 Swiss francs).[4]

Have all the rich people left those countries, and did their economy or society become unstable? This is what critics of a wealth tax often argue will happen. No, they did not. In fact, Switzerland is a haven for many of the world's wealthy. Many even go to extreme lengths to be admitted as citizens, knowing full well they will be subject to a wealth tax.

Evidence from the rest of the world shows that if politicians want to implement a wealth tax, they can. In December 2020, Argentina's legislators passed a new wealth tax to pay for expenses incurred because of COVID-19. The legislation imposed a tax at a progressive rate of up to 3.5 per cent on wealth inside the country and up to 5.25 per cent on wealth held outside Argentina. This applied to roughly 12,000 people with assets worth more than $2.7 million CAD (200 million pesos). The money recouped by this one-off wealth tax was split among several priorities:

- 20 per cent to medical supplies
- 20 per cent to relief for small- and medium-sized businesses
- 20 per cent to student scholarships
- 15 per cent to social developments, and
- the remaining 25 per cent to natural gas ventures.

The Argentinian government hoped to raise $4.13 billion CAD (300 billion pesos) from the 12,000 richest citizens of a well-off country of 40 million.[5]

Across the world, many political leaders, organizations, and economists are leading the fight to implement a similar wealth tax in their countries. As Indiana University law professor David Gamage explained, "All around the world you see increasing awareness of growing wealth and income inequalities, combined with growing awareness that our tax system is not up to dealing with this problem."[6]

United States Senator Elizabeth Warren proposed a 2 per cent wealth tax on every dollar of a person's net worth over $50 million and an additional 1 per cent tax on every dollar in net worth over $1 billion. Senator Bernie Sanders said he would impose an even higher top tax rate of 8 per cent on fortunes over $10 billion. These tax rates would apply to a US citizen's wealth held anywhere in the world, and Senator Warren proposed an "exit tax" of 40 per cent if someone wanted to forsake their US citizenship to avoid paying the wealth tax.

A wealth tax commission in the UK — led by a team of former senior civil servants, tax experts, and economists — issued a final report in December 2020, proposing that the country impose a temporary wealth tax payable on all individual wealth above $861,000 CAD (£500,000) and charged at 1 per cent a year for five years. This tax, they concluded, would be highly beneficial for the country and would raise up to $430 billion CAD in five years (£250 billion). The commission found that this measure would help with "sharing the burden of paying for the crisis across those with the broadest shoulders."[7]

The rising global interest in wealth taxes seems to stem from the startling realization of the extreme differences in wealth and the negative impacts of an ultra-unequal world. COVID-19 showed that we are not all in this together. Many of the super-wealthy benefited from the pandemic as they reaped profits from the work of low-wage workers. Meanwhile, workers were exposed to the virus at work, on public transit, and at home. In contrast, the wealthy used their money to shield themselves and put others at risk with expensive vacations in tropical locales. COVID-19 exacerbated the widespread public feeling that our system isn't fair and that the game is rigged against most people. The upswell of pressure made some decision-makers consider taxing wealth when facing the issue of how to pay the pandemic costs and the recovery.

Implementing a wealth tax, temporary or ongoing, is feasible and realistic. What should it look like in Canada?

A Wealth Tax in Canada

When considering the criteria for a wealth tax, we must choose carefully to avoid unwanted effects. As in a good recipe, we must find the right balance to ensure the measure will be as effective and fair as possible. The NDP was the first federal party in Canada to come out in favour of a wealth tax. Its proposed 1 per cent wealth tax would apply to families with wealth above $20 million, and would be levied annually on their net worth above that threshold.

Real estate, luxury items, and investments they own would all be taxed; only wealth won in lotteries would be exempt.

In concrete terms, a household with total wealth of $30 million would pay an extra $100,000 per year in taxes — 1 per cent of the household's wealth over $20 million. The federal NDP decided to tax households rather than individuals, to avoid a scenario where one spouse just passes half their wealth to another to avoid the tax. The NDP also chose the 1 per cent rate to avoid the tax becoming an incentive for these super-wealthy people to move to a country with no such tax. At the 1 per cent rate, the measure meets the desired objectives, but it also prevents a plausible problem: given the low cost to those affected, it becomes more expensive for them to leave the country than to stay and pay the tax. In other words, it's a well-balanced recipe.

In his independent report evaluating this proposal, the Parliamentary Budget Officer estimated that 13,800 households in Canada would be subject to this tax. This means that only 0.1 per cent of Canadians would pay more — truly a tax paid only by the super-wealthy. Most of us probably don't even know anyone who would come close to paying this tax.

People often agree with the principle of a wealth tax, but ask whether the richest won't find a way to avoid paying this tax just as they avoid paying existing ones. The question is legitimate and important to examine and answer, but first we offer a caution: beware of people, corporations, or political parties that frame avoidance of new taxes as inevitable. It's often in their interest to convince us that this problem cannot be fixed, therefore the corrective measure is not worth doing because it won't be effective. To address the avoidance problem, a wealth tax must come with clear legislation, tough enforcement against tax evasion, transparency on the real (often called "beneficial") ownership of corporations in Canada, and penalties for multimillionaires who try to avoid paying. All these elements must work hand in hand to make a wealth tax — actually any tax — effective.

The Canada Revenue Agency (CRA) is the organization in charge of ensuring the integrity of our tax system. It's Canada's government agency that fights tax evasion and avoidance tactics. Under the NDP's plan, the CRA would conduct regular and comprehensive audits to review all types of assets covered by the wealth tax: real estate, cars, luxury items, etc. Because the number of households affected by the measure is so small, the agency could conceivably go into greater depth in its audits to ensure the truth and accuracy of all information provided.

Instead of relying on self-declaration regarding the value of an asset, the CRA could use third-party-reported information to determine values. The agency already does this in other areas of the tax system. For example, if an individual attempted to reduce the value of a $100,000 luxury car by claiming it was worth $75,000, the CRA could verify the actual value using third-party information. The government would not just take the word of the super-wealthy on how much they're worth — someone would check. On top of that, there would be penalties to deter people from taking assets out of the country to avoid the tax.

In the 2020 Saskatchewan election, the provincial NDP proposed a similar annual net wealth tax. Its version, along the lines of Elizabeth Warren's proposal, would have applied the tax to a household's global wealth, thus discouraging the movement of assets to avoid paying the wealth tax.

These accountability and enforcement measures are extremely important because, as we have seen, the super-rich will do everything they can to pay as little tax as possible. Unlike the rest of us, they can also afford the best tax experts to find ways to get around the rules.

Another note of caution: there is an ongoing supply of disinformation regarding wealth taxes coming from right-wing think tanks and economists. Thus, you might hear that "the amount recouped will be small" or "the tax won't even raise the amount projected" or — the perennial favourite — "it's way too complex."

In fact, the Parliamentary Budget Officer estimated that a 1 per cent tax on Canada's wealthiest would generate nearly $70 billion in new revenue over ten years, rising from $5.6 billion in year one to $9.5 billion in year ten.[8] The revenues generated increase year after year partially because the PBO foresees that the government would be better and better at enforcing the tax and that the richest would have less and less opportunity to avoid it.

This estimate is actually conservative because it still includes an assumption that the rich will avoid about one-third of the theoretical increase through tax avoidance strategies. Alex Hemingway, an economist with the Canadian Centre for Policy Alternatives, has estimated that the tax could raise as much as $10 billion in its first year.[9] This reflects a calculation that the wealthiest Canadians together have at least a trillion dollars in assets. So $5.6 billion is a low number that already assumes the tax will not be collected at 100 per cent of its capacity.

The same PBO reported that the administrative cost of such a measure would be $144 million for the first year — which it deducted when it estimated the potential revenue of the measure. So, despite what the economic elite and its lobbyists and advocates may say, a wealth tax not only is feasible in Canada, but would also be extremely beneficial for the Canadian government.

We note again that, after a certain point, the accumulation of wealth no longer makes a difference to a wealthy person — $100,000 more or less will not prevent them from getting what they want. The super-wealthy are way past that. This includes all the luxury items and privileges that they have become accustomed to, which are already far from anything that could remotely be thought of as essential needs. Extreme wealth only grows and grows until transferred to another family member. Most of the money is never used, and could never conceivably be used productively in a single person's lifetime. Often, exclusive real estate is the chosen path to benefit future generations. Philanthropy can be used to improve the image of extreme wealth hoarders and allow them to keep the system that benefits them in place.

Take David Thomson and family, Canadians who own and control a media and publishing empire founded by David's grandfather, Roy Thomson. The family's wealth was estimated at $50.6 billion in September 2020, a jump of $8.8 billion from the beginning of the pandemic. Forbes lists David as the thirty-third richest person in the world, but Bloomberg estimates that the family's wealth is split among David, his two siblings, and four cousins.

Even split among seven people, this amount is difficult to wrap our heads around. If you lived for 100 years and spent $1 million every day of your life, you'd still have money left over. This, at the same time that there are nearly five million people living in poverty in the same country. Years of tax cuts and austerity have helped the Thomson family accumulate this wealth and left too many of the rest of us with insecure jobs, inadequate housing, and a failing social safety net. We risk the tax cut/austerity dynamic happening again if we don't organize to ensure that our governments choose a different path.

The NDP's wealth tax proposal would ask each Thomson heir to pay 1 per cent of their wealth over $20 million, a family total of $505 million a year, to the federal government. This amount alone would cover the cost of eliminating interest on all federal student loans in Canada. In this way, it would put more money into the pockets of young people who are struggling to make ends meet, and who face a weaker labour market after the pandemic as well as the increasing impact of climate change.

Yet this tax would not prevent David Thomson or his family from getting all the luxury items they want and the inevitable peace of mind that must come with this surreal amount of wealth. We should also remember that this wealth has been created and has grown because of workers, consumers, and public infrastructure. For us and many experts, there is no doubt that this tax is the way forward.

Why a Wealth Tax in Canada?

Here are the key reasons why we should have a wealth tax in Canada.

Reason No. 1 — A Wealth Tax Would Provide a Significant Source of Government Revenues

There are many wealthy families in Canada who are not paying their fair share, so there is a substantial amount of money to be collected and redistributed. At the same time, there are many areas that require investments; these will continue to grow as a result of the pandemic and climate crisis. The NDP's plan for a wealth tax has the potential to bring in at least $5.6 billion every year. This is a significant amount of revenue that the government could use to repair damage to public services while supporting the postpandemic recovery in an inclusive way.

COVID-19 has required the federal government to spend a substantial amount of money to support people in Canada. Although this was the right thing to do, many Canadians expect that it will eventually lead to more cuts to balance things out. A new source of revenue provided by a wealth tax could prevent governments from placing the burden on the middle and working classes by cutting once again into public services.

While some economists were predicting that the economy would bounce back to nearly normal once the pandemic ran its course, this seemed unlikely at the time of writing. The federal government might need to continue to spend considerable amounts of money to support the recovery, so ensuring an added and regular source or revenue seems like the smart and prudent thing to do. Furthermore, knowing that this will not be our last pandemic, we need to make significant investments in public health and other social infrastructure to ensure we are not caught off guard when a future crisis of this magnitude arrives. Make no mistake: it's a matter of *when*, not *if*.

At each crisis, austerity and government cutbacks hover over the middle and working classes. As soon as investments and deficits expand out of the ordinary, the defenders of "keep our house in order" surface to push their agenda of small government and opposition to state intervention. In the past, both Liberals and Conservatives have taken advantage of the situation to cut public services while at the same time giving tax cuts to the economic elite. A wealth tax has the potential to provide the government with considerable additional revenues. It serves partly to fight the arguments for austerity, while contributing to rebalancing the inequality in Canadian society.

Reason No. 2 — A Wealth Tax Has Broad Support

As we discussed earlier, interest in a wealth tax to tackle extreme wealth is growing globally. Many leading economists, unions, and organizations that have long fought for greater tax justice support the idea. Globally, world-renowned economists like Thomas Piketty, Emmanuel Saez, Gabriel Zucman, and Nobel Prize winners Joseph Stiglitz and Paul Krugman are among its strongest proponents. They explain that although other changes to the tax system are also crucial, a wealth tax tackles the causes of economic inequality in a unique way. As US Senator Elizabeth Warren said about American tax laws, "Our tax code focuses on taxing income, but a family's wealth is also an important measure of how much it has benefited from the economy and its ability to pay taxes. And judged against wealth, our tax system asks the rich to pay a lot less than everyone else."[10] In other words, the wealth tax tackles the same problem as the other essential measures we will discuss later, but from a different angle.

In Canada, organizations like Canadians for Tax Fairness, the Broadbent Institute, and the Canadian Centre for Policy Alternatives and economists like Toby Sanger and Andrew Jackson are leading the fight for a wealth tax. The idea is also supported by a group called Resource Movement, a community of young people with wealth that is working toward redistribution of wealth, land, and power in Canada. In 2020, the editorial board of the *Toronto Star* also expressed interest, saying a wealth tax was worth considering.[11]

Public opinion polls in 2020 showed considerable support for a wealth tax among the Canadian public, and among voters supporting all federal political parties. A November 2020 survey by Abacus Data showed that the NDP proposal of a 1 per cent tax on wealth of people who have more than $20 million in net assets was supported by 79 per cent of Canadians, including 35 per cent who strongly favoured it. The survey found that 87 per cent of NDP voters supported the proposal, along with 93 per cent of Bloc voters, 86 per cent of Liberal voters, 85 per cent of Green voters, and 64 per cent of Conservative voters.[12] With such broad cross-party support from voters, it is surprising that members of partliament from all parties except the Green Party voted against the federal NDP's motion to implement a wealth tax and an excess profit tax in November 2020.[13]

Reason No. 3 — A Wealth Tax Could Help the Social Climate

The social impacts that result from extreme inequalities should not be understated. Feelings of injustice and of being a victim in a rigged system are increasing among Canadians, and these feelings can encourage social movements that have the potential to be very dangerous. They can lead to individual or mass radicalization, social instability, or even revolt. Some politicians have found it advantageous to stoke feelings of resentment among their supporters, and use these feelings to stigmatize certain groups (such as people of immigrant background, a particular religion, or a particular skin colour), or to introduce dangerous and totally unfounded conspiracy theories.

Income and wealth inequality allows these movement leaders and politicians to cloak their unacceptable messages of white supremacy in the language of economic insecurity, obscuring the issues of both economic and racial inequality and distracting from effective solutions to both problems. All of these phenomena pose a risk of social fracturing and can lead to the erosion of democratic institutions and processes in Canada, just as they do in the US. The Proud Boys and other extreme Canadian groups are largely drawn from a white educated middle class, and they have been effective at pushing conservative politicians in Canada further and further toward a politics of mistrust and division.

A wealth tax would help restore more justice in our tax system and alleviate legitimate frustrations and discouragements that might drive voters to support this political rhetoric. It is an extremely disturbing experience to live in fear of not making it to your next paycheque or having to choose between food and medicine. Being regularly reminded that many families are taking advantage of offshore tax havens and rules written in their favour within Canada only makes it worse. Addressing these obvious inequities can help to avoid the social fractures they cause. Failing to do so will reinforce the alienation and sense that the system is rigged.

Reason No. 4 — A Wealth Tax Does a Better Job Than Alternatives like an Inheritance Tax

Some critics argue that if we reformed our tax system based on labour and capital income, we could achieve the same result as a wealth tax. Others tell us that we should implement an inheritance tax instead, as that will be perceived as fairer to tax wealth as it transitions from one generation to the next.

We believe that a wealth tax addresses the injustices of our tax system in a very specific way that cannot be accomplished through the income-based tax system. Years of gaps in our taxation and worker and environmental protection have allowed extreme accumulation of wealth, as we have seen. There is no mechanism that would allow us to recover any part of this wealth other than the wealth tax. If, for example, we increase the income tax rate on top earners to make it more progressive, which we believe should be done as well, it will only apply to future income, not on wealth the super-rich already own. In other words, the wealth tax is an important tool to compensate for the low tax rate on the super-rich of the last century and to tackle out of control growth in wealth for the wealthiest. This is something we cannot achieve with a capital gains tax or the income tax.[14]

As of 2021, Canada, unlike many other countries, had no taxes on inheritances or gifts. Provincial probate fees on estates are set at comparatively low rates and can be fairly easily avoided through tax-planning measures. The absence of such taxes makes for "stronger arguments for having a net wealth tax,"[15] said the OECD.

An inheritance tax and a wealth tax do not achieve the same results. An inheritance tax is only paid when the inheritance is transferred — more often than not, when a person dies and the wealth is transferred to a family member. The tax is not levied on an annual basis. Consequently, it allows extreme fortunes to grow tax-free for many years. Moreover, in a context where many of the wealthiest people are relatively young, it may take time before any tax is collected. These aspects also complicate government financial planning in Canada, since the revenues from an inheritance tax are very difficult to predict.

Although a wealth tax alone will of course not solve all problems, it is an essential tool to fight against economic inequalities by correcting the very low rate of overall taxation on large fortunes and by bringing government more revenues to be used to invest in people and support an equitable and prosperous economy for us all.

Conclusion

Discussion surrounding a wealth tax for Canada continues. Although there is growing support for the measure, the more serious and popular the idea becomes, the more we will hear from critics. Neoliberal economists, right-wing think tanks, and the economic elite — essentially those who have held power for decades — will use every tool at their disposal to discourage policy-makers from implementing such a measure. That's why it will be crucial for the rest of us to organize, because with the strength of numbers we can achieve progressive policies.

We cannot let status quo advocates divide us with discredited economic myths that have been repeatedly contradicted by research — if we do, the challenge will be much more difficult. We hope that in this chapter we have given you sufficient background to explain why a wealth tax would be a fair and successful new tax for Canada. We know from opinion polls that most Canadians support the idea. But it will take active engagement from many people across the country to counter the pressure coming from the wealthy and their behind-the-scenes supporters to make this a reality. We all need to work together to make it happen.

CHAPTER 5

CLOSING TAX LOOPHOLES

The Canadian tax system includes built-in features that mainly benefit the wealthiest. These reflect past government decisions to allow the super-rich to use tax planning to avoid paying their fair share. Some of these measures ensure that returns to capital are taxed at a lower rate than other income, and some allow the one per cent to send their wealth to countries with very low tax rates, known as tax havens. In other words, governments in the past have put in place unfair tax laws and rules that allow the wealthiest to continue to get richer, while the rest of us are left to pay our taxes in full. Unsurprisingly, this contributes directly to Canada's growing inequality while also depriving governments of much-needed revenues to fund health and social programs — all the more so in a post-COVID-19 recovery world.

In this chapter we focus on three well-known loopholes in our tax system that help Canada's richest get rich and stay rich. The effects of each have been documented and calculated. Each one confers special benefits on the one per cent. Some other

Canadians benefit from these loopholes too, but less so. Only the wealthiest derive benefits worth millions — sometimes tens or even hundreds of millions — from these three loopholes. Nevertheless, the loopholes have existed for years, often decades, and any efforts to shut them down have been ineffective.

Loophole No. 1 — Special Treatment for Capital Gains
How Does it Work?

"Capital gains" are profits you make when you sell an asset (that's the "capital") and get more for it than it cost you (that's the "gain"). This happens most often when people sell shares or real estate, but of course there are lots of ways to make capital gains. The money made from capital gains is just as good as the money made from employment income, but Canada's tax laws treat capital gains income differently from salaries, wages and other types of employment income. For people with lots of assets, capital gains can provide a considerable source of income.

According to Canada's tax laws as of 2021, profits made on some kinds of assets — the house you own and live in, registered investments (Registered Retirement Savings Plans [RRSPs], Tax Free Savings Accounts [TFSAs] and Registered Education Savings Plans [RESPs]) and small businesses — are not included in taxable capital gains. For those assets that are included, people who make capital gains are taxed on only 50 per cent of what they made. In contrast, people with employment income are taxed on almost all of their income. So if you invested in real estate, buying a property for $300,000 and later selling it for $350,000, the government will consider that you realized a capital gain of $50,000. Yet instead of adding $50,000 to your income the year you sold the real estate, you are allowed to add only half of your profit to your income. So only $25,000 would be considered taxable income that you would include on your annual income tax return. Essentially, only $25,000 counts as income and you have just made the other $25,000 completely tax-free.

It hasn't always been like that. This tax loophole was greatly enlarged in 2000, as one of a series of measures put in place to favour the richest people. The cover story for the change was that these wealthy people would then invest more and grow the economy and create jobs. Reducing taxes on investment profits was supposed to benefit all of us through the "trickle-down" effect.

This tax cut for the rich came after years of cuts in services and social programs for the working and middle classes. We were told that the government needed to temporarily tighten its belt through the 1990s to get a debt and deficit crisis under control. But when we got through the debt crisis by the end of the nineties, Canadians found ourselves with a permanent reduction in the size and capacity of the government to provide critical public services. But the one per cent got tax changes that allowed them to accumulate even more wealth.

One of the steep cuts in taxes for the wealthy introduced in 2000 was a change in tax on capital gains income. While the percentage of capital gains that had been counted as income had varied over time, in 2000 it stood at 75 per cent. This meant that if you had made a capital gain of $50,000 as in our example above, $37,500 would have been included as income on your annual tax return. The cut to including only 50 per cent of capital gains led to a huge reduction in government revenues. It amounted to a significant gift to Canada's super-wealthy.

What's the Problem?

There are several problems with treating money earned from capital gains differently from money earned from other sources, such as employment. The first problem is justice. Depending on how you make your money, you will be taxed very differently. This flies in the face of the principle that has guided tax reform in Canada since the 1967 Report of the Royal Commission on Taxation. Kenneth Carter, the commission chair, had a simple and memorable way of explaining what constitutes fair and just taxes: "A buck is a buck is a buck." His royal commission's final report recommended full 100 per cent inclusion of money made through capital gains in income tax.[1]

Here's why a special low rate for money made from capital gains is unfair and unjust. A person who strikes it rich with their investments pays income tax on only half of their gains when they are sold. At the same time, a nurse who works mandatory overtime to care for COVID-19 patients will have her entire salary taxed. How can it be fair that the investor's income should be taxed at a lower rate than the nurse's income?

Remember that the cover story used to justify the low rate was that, in the end, investors receiving capital gains would use the money for investments that would "trickle down" to create growth and good jobs. Now, as we have already discussed, investors' wealth does not "trickle down." David Macdonald, the senior economist at the Canadian Center for Policy Alternatives and a frequent media expert on income inequality issues in Canada, explains this way: "It seems only fair that whether a person earns an income working or when they sell stock, the tax system should treat that individual income the same."[2]

The second problem with a special low rate on capital gains is that it exacerbates inequality. There is excellent research, published in the scholarly *Canadian Tax Journal* by three experts including Brian B. Murphy of Statistics Canada, which documents the results of this tax loophole. Their research produced definitive findings: over 88 per cent of the value of this tax loophole goes to the one per cent[3] — that is, people making an annual income of $236,000 and up. This is the primary group who get a lot of capital gains from investments. For some Canadians in the one per cent, capital gains comprise a substantial portion of their income — yet only half that high income is taxed thanks to this loophole.

In 2017, the federal government itself reported that the total cost of this loophole to Ottawa was $10.2 billion.[4] Of that amount, almost $9 billion went to benefit people in the top one per cent. This is a clear and simple example of how the tax system is rigged.

The third problem with the special low tax rate on capital gains is that this loophole can be used by corporations and companies large and small. According to the federal government's own data, this loophole costs an additional $9.6 billion when used by corporate entities.

When we combine the cost of this measure for individuals and corporations, we end up with an astonishing $19.9 billion in taxes going unpaid every year — and adding to the wealth of the already wealthy one per cent.[5]

The Solution

In the 2019 election, the federal NDP proposed a return to the 75 per cent rate for money earned from capital gains — back to the rate that was in place before the federal Liberal government cut it in 2000. This is a simple and straightforward step. It's not as simple and straightforward to talk about, though, since the actual amount of income tax that someone will pay on their capital gains depends on their total taxable income and their top marginal tax bracket.

Here's an example of what it would be like: Someone who buys $20,000 in stock and then later sells it for $30,000 would have a capital gain of $10,000. At the 50 per cent rate, only half of that amount, or $5,000, would be included as taxable income.

This $5,000 will then be taxed according to the bracket they are in when we consider all of their taxable income. If the individual was in the top one per cent of income earners and made over $200,000 a year, their top marginal tax bracket is 33 per cent. They would pay 33 per cent tax on $5,000, which works out to a total of $1,650. From the original $10,000 profit, they will be taxed only $1,650.

If we raise the capital gains inclusion rate to 75 per cent, then our investor would include $7,500 of capital gains income on their income tax return. At a top marginal tax rate of 33 per cent, this person would have to pay $2,475 in taxes, an increase of $825. This might not seem like a notable difference, but this one change would allow the government to receive an average of $9.5 billion per year more in tax revenues, as estimated by the Parliamentary Budget Officer.[6]

Because of our progressive income tax system, if the $10,000 capital gain was an individual's only income, for example a retiree selling stocks to pay for housing, they wouldn't pay any income tax on that money in either scenario. So while people not in the top one per cent of income earners do get a small portion of the total impact of the low rate on capital gains, the lower your overall income, the less this change impacts you.

By reforming this loophole that mostly benefits the richest one per cent to give the government more money to reinvest in programs that benefit the entire population, we would make a small dent in economic inequality, which is good for our social climate and our economy.

There would be other benefits too. Changing the rules of the tax on capital gains would help significantly in curbing real estate speculation. If we reduce the incentive for people to buy houses on speculation, it should help cool down the housing market in cities like Toronto, Vancouver and many other places in Canada, where the dream of buying a home for young people has become simply unattainable.

Who's against It, and Why?

This tax loophole can work for Canadians who are not in the one per cent. As just noted, a small investor who makes some money from buying and selling a rental property or a few shares in a fast-rising company can cash in their investment and treat the money they make as a capital gain. When they do, they pay half the tax they would pay if the money came to them as a bonus at work. So small investors and financial advisors helping people save for their retirement wouldn't like this change.

Whenever the subject of capital gains comes up, concerns get raised about small business owners, farmers, or homeowners being treated unfairly. Small business owners and farmers often plan to use the capital they have accumulated as an alternative to a pension. Anyone who owns a house in Canada purchased more than a year or two ago is likely to see that they would receive a big capital gain when they sell their house, and so might be concerned about a change in this tax.

Canada's tax laws already take these concerns into account. Capital gains from sales of small businesses, family farms and owner-occupied homes are already exempted from tax. Raising the rate from 50 to 75 per cent wouldn't affect these groups. By this single change, and without touching the exemptions, the federal government would receive another $9.5 billion to invest in needed social programs every year.

The one per cent have not been vocal in opposing a change that would narrow this loophole, even though it is worth $8.8 billion to them every year. Increasing the rate from 50 to 75 per cent would reduce their after-tax income by half that amount, or $4.4 billion. But perhaps it's not surprising that Canada's wealthy are not going public with their objections to paying more tax on their capital gains. With their many connections to the Liberal and Conservative parties, they can make their arguments in private.

Corporate interests opposed to this change will also try to distract us from the large beneficiaries and point to smaller businesses such as smaller-scale residential landlords who might be impacted by this change. Since capital gains tax only applies when the capital is sold and a gain on the initial investment is made, changing the rate would have no impact on the day-to-day functioning of these businesses. It only comes into play when a real profit from the sale of an asset has been made.

How Changing the Capital Gains Exemption Will Help Share the Wealth in Canada

It's true that this loophole allows many people who are not in the one per cent to pay less tax than they would with the rate set at 75 per cent, or at the 100 per cent rate, which would fully implement the principle that "a buck is a buck is a buck." Since no one likes to pay more tax, the champions of the one per cent can count on others to resist a reduction of this loophole. There are lots of small investors who pay less tax thanks to the 50 per cent rule.

We should keep in mind that those small investors, all together, benefit to the tune of about $700 million in taxes they don't pay in an average year. Raising the rate to 75 per cent will cost those small investors a small additional amount in taxes in years when they receive capital gains. On the other hand, there are the relatively few Canadians — numbering fewer than 290,000 — with annual incomes above $236,000 who benefit to the tune of $4.4 billion annually. The single step of shrinking this loophole will have a major effect on many of those in the one per cent who receive the lion's share of all capital gains every year. It will slow down the growth in their wealth, give the government much needed revenue and contribute to reducing inequality.

Loophole No. 2 — Stock Options

What Is It?

The stock options loophole was adopted in 1977 to help small emerging companies. The original idea was that a company could promise its employees that they would be able to purchase a given number of its shares at a specific price some time in the future. The price promised to employees is set lower than the expected future value of the share. The benefit is that employees can, at a future date, purchase and own part of the company at a discount. Or the employee can purchase the shares in the future at the lower price, then sell them at the market price and make an immediate capital gain.

The idea was that this type of compensation also encouraged these employees to dedicate more time to the company's success, considering that they could earn extra money on top of their salaries when the value of the company's shares increased. Offering this deal to potential employees was also designed to help startups attract talent to grow the company before it had enjoyed enough success to have the revenue to pay competitive salaries.

Here's an example of how this works: A company promises some of its employees that they can buy company shares at 10 cents — lower than what everyone expects the market value of the stock will be. Employees may exercise this stock option at any given time during the agreement, but they are not required to do so. Meanwhile the market value is 25 cents. An employee could buy the shares at 10 cents and then immediately resell the shares and receive a capital gain of 15 cents per share. As we remember from the previous section, only 50 per cent of this capital gain is taxed. Using this loophole, money received from employee stock options is taxed as if it is a capital gain (50 per cent deduction) rather than as income.

What's the Problem?

Unfortunately, this measure has been hijacked by the one per cent. Though it was initially designed to help raise money for startups and expansion, this tool is now primarily used by Canada's ultra-rich. This fact was acknowledged in the Liberal platform in both 2011 and 2015. Yet as of early 2021, the problem remained.

Canadians for Tax Fairness, one of the leading organizations fighting for a fairer tax system, has analyzed this loophole and summarized its findings this way:

> *The justification for the stock options deduction when it was introduced was that it would help struggling companies get on their feet by encouraging employee co-ownership through stock options. But that's not who is cashing in. Over 90% of the benefit goes to the top 1% of income earners.*[7]

It's not hard to identify many of the individuals who benefit the most from using this loophole. The ten highest-income corporate CEOs received $60 million in stock options in 2017, along with their salaries, share awards and other forms of compensation.[8]

- Richard Baker of Hudson's Bay topped the list. His salary was a healthy $861,000, but stock options added $16,625,000 to his take for the year. When other forms of compensation were added in, his total compensation for the year was $54,847,131.
- Second on the list was Donald J. Walker, CEO of the car parts company Magna International. His salary was $422,045, but that was only the beginning of what he received. For him, stock options were worth an additional $6,181,336. With all forms of compensation taken together, his total for the year was $26,436,899.
- Keith Creel, CEO of the Canadian Pacific Railway, had a base salary of $1.4 million in 2017, but that paled in comparison with his stock option remuneration of $10,516,830.

The startup rationale for the stock option loophole dissolves as soon as we look at this list of winners. Hudson's Bay, established in 1670, is three and a half centuries away from being a startup. Magna was a startup — in the 1950s. And most Canadians learned about the history of the Canadian Pacific Railway in school — it was a startup in 1881. All in all, stock options make up about 22 per cent of the total compensation of the top one hundred CEOs in Canada.[9]

Government statistics from 2017 help illustrate this further:

- 2,330 Canadians with an annual income of over $1 million claimed, on average, a stock option deduction of $577,000 — in total they claimed deductions of $1.34 billion.[10]
- 94 per cent of the benefit that year went to the one per cent.
- This measure cost the government $655 million that year — meaning that $615 million went to the top one per cent because of that loophole.[11]
- Put another way, the government failed to collect that $615 million to spread Canada's wealth through social programs that would improve the lives of everyone.

The stock option loophole is also used by some for what was intended. In fact, another 34,300 Canadians benefited from the stock option loophole in 2017. There were 20,140 with annual incomes below $200,000 whose average stock option deduction was $6,000, and another 14,160 with annual incomes between $200,000 and $1 million whose average amount was $44,000. The total stock option deductions for these employees was $750 million — itself a sizable amount, and the cost to the government in taxes that would have otherwise been paid was $375 million. But at least this amount was in line with the supposed original purpose of this loophole.

Besides contributing to inequality and reducing the ability of government to provide needed social services, a tax measure that gives a bonus to CEOs when the price of their company's shares goes up has other effects as well. Some economists point out that linking big business executives' income to share prices creates an incentive for them to concentrate on actions that will boost prices in the short term, at the expense of actions that could benefit the company in the long term. Providing a tax incentive for this type of income can encourage corporate leaders to lose focus on what is important for the long-term prosperity of their companies.

Despite all the evidence that it benefits mostly the one per cent, successive Liberal and Conservative governments lost billions of dollars in tax revenue over the past three decades through this loophole. Even though the Liberals admitted to the problem and promised to fix it in 2011 and 2015, they haven't. After being pressured by the economic elite, the Liberals dropped their first plan to address this loophole in 2016.[12] In 2019, in his final budget before he resigned, Liberal Finance Minister Bill Morneau announced a cap of $200,000 on the stock option loophole.

This change was supposed to come into effect in January 2020, but again the Liberals postponed it until July 2021. After the Liberals yielded three times to the pressure of rich CEOs, it would be legitimate to believe that these changes will never be implemented and the Liberals will simply continue to campaign on them. Furthermore, their proposal is inadequate. It would still allow millionaires to claim a stock option deduction on their first $200,000. If we take the numbers from 2017, this would mean that the Liberals would still give around $233 million to 2,330 ultra-rich Canadians, instead of just eliminating that loophole for them.

The Liberal's proposed changes would not impact people with income between $200,000 and $1 million because on average they claimed $44,000 — way below the cap. In other words, this is a typical strategy to make it look as if a change is progressive, without actually addressing the inherent unfairness. The proposed changes will not alter the fact that the one per cent will benefit more, but the Liberals will be able to claim to have done something. For context, the Parliamentary Budget Officer has estimated that the measure proposed by the Liberal government would not raise any revenue until 2032 or 2033 and that amount would only be $144 million.[13]

The Solution

This stands in a stark contrast with the NDP proposal. The Parliamentary Budget Officer estimated that, if the NDP solution was implemented, the government would recoup $140 million in year one, progressively increasing to $1 billion in year eight — an average of $489 million per year.[14] In eight years, the NDP's proposal would bring in $4 billion in new revenue for the federal government, while the Liberals' proposal would bring in only a tenth of that amount — roughly $400 million.

The solution the NDP proposes is quite simple: close this loophole completely and work with startups to determine how the government can support them without creating an incentive that can be abused by more established corporations and their executives. And it can be done, if we have a government that has the courage to stand up to rich CEOs.

Loophole No. 3 — Business Entertainment Expenses

What Is It?

This tax loophole allows all businesses to deduct up to 50 per cent of the cost of meals and entertainment for their clients from their taxable income. Of course, businesses have the ability to deduct many of their expenses before calculating their net income (or profit) on which they pay taxes. This specific tax rule allows a business to deduct 50 per cent of the amount they spend on an event to entertain their clients. So, if a business entertainment event costs a company $1,000, the company can deduct only $500 from its taxable income.

Allowable expenses that can be deducted include food, beverages and tickets and entrance fees to concerts or sporting events. Tips, cover charges, room rentals to provide entertainment, such as hospitality suites, and the cost of private boxes at sports facilities are also deductible. The cost of entertaining guests at clubs, cruises, vacations and similar trips can all be deducted at a rate of 50 per cent.

The Problem

The problem, as you can imagine, is that while the law stipulates that business must be conducted at these events for them to be eligible for the deduction, it is really hard for the Canada Revenue Agency to know for sure whether this actually happens. This leads to abuse by big corporations that routinely deduct entertainment expenses, regardless of whether business is actually being conducted.

The distinguished Osgoode Hall tax law professor Neil Brooks once quipped about this loophole: “There is more tax fraud taking place at one Blue Jays baseball game than all the welfare fraud in Ontario in a whole year.”[15]

While this measure can be useful for small businesses in attracting clients and even rewarding employees, it is simply outrageous that large and highly profitable companies like the Royal Bank of Canada or Bell are able to deduct expenses for entertainment. Since this measure is widely abused by large corporations and is difficult to audit, it helps many large corporations pay less tax. So those of us who don't avoid taxes end up paying more, since the entertainment loophole cost the public purse a total of $505 million in 2017.[16]

The Solution

The solution for this loophole is simple: eliminate it for all big companies and allow small businesses and self-employed workers to use it.

This simple step, according to the independent Parliamentary Budget Officer who analyzed its effect, would generate at least $468 million in additional revenues from large businesses and corporations. In other words, another half billion that can be reinvested in social programs for everyone in Canada.

Who's against It, and Why

The business entertainment expense loophole has applied to businesses of every size. For small businesses and self-employed workers, it recognizes that the costs of business lunches, golf games and similar activities are important to maintaining good relations with customers, suppliers and other business associates. Small businesses and self-employed workers are limited on what they spend on these items by their size and financial capacity. Understandably, the business community and all its organizations don't want to lose access to this loophole.

Big companies and corporations can quietly lobby for this loophole behind the scenes, without emphasizing how sizable the benefit they receive. Restricting this loophole to self-employed workers and small businesses leaves only those large companies and corporations to oppose the change.

Conclusion

It's not just one loophole or one cut in taxes on the wealthy that led us to a Canada where most of the increase in our country's wealth has gone to the top one per cent, while working- and middle-class Canadians see little improvement in their own lives.

In this chapter we have focused on only three loopholes that increase the wealth of the already wealthy, while depriving the government of funds that could pay for measures that would improve the lives of all Canadians. With just these three changes, we came up with an additional $10.5 billion in annual revenue for the federal government.

These solutions only need legislation to be adopted, and the NDP has already developed and proposed legislation to do this in the House of Commons. During COVID-19, we saw how legislation could be quickly passed and implemented, if political parties wanted to. If there is one thing that COVID-19 demonstrated, it is that when a government wants to take action, it can do so.

Closing tax loopholes, starting with these three, would be a major step toward giving the government more tax revenues — and beginning to reduce the drastic inequality that has arisen in Canada in the last four decades. It would mark progress in sharing the wealth of a country that is wealthy but has allowed far too much of that wealth to be concentrated in the hands of a few.

CHAPTER 6

INCREASING INCOME TAXES FOR THE ONE PER CENT

Income inequality and wealth inequality are closely linked, and the higher up we go, the more extreme it gets. To be in the top 0.01 per cent in Canada, your total pre-tax income had to be at least $3.9 million per year. In 2018, there were 2,800 individuals in Canada whose total reported income was at least that high. An annual income of $3.9 million works out to a hefty $75,000 a week — and remember, that's the minimum these 2,800 individuals were receiving. Many were receiving considerably more, every week.

To be in Canada's one per cent, you had to have a total pre-tax income of at least $270,000 in 2018. To be in the top 10 per cent, you had to have an income of $100,000.

These incomes at the top are markedly higher than the average amounts earned by other Canadians, and this gap between the highest-income Canadians and everyone else has grown dramatically over the past forty years. As the chart from Statistics Canada shows, those in the top 10 per cent have seen their

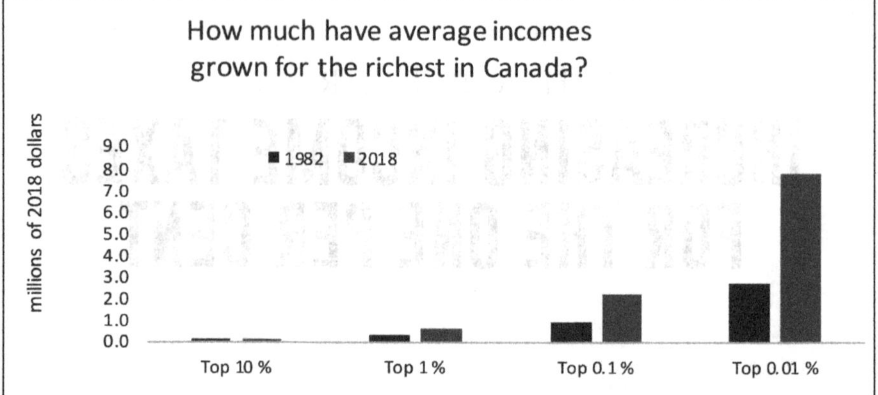

Average total income including capital gains, from Statistics Canada. Table 11-10-0055-01 High income tax filers in Canada

incomes grow somewhat in the years from 1982 to 2018. But the further up you go, the bigger the increase.

The table shows that even after we adjust for inflation, the top 0.01 per cent have seen their average pre-tax incomes grow from about \$2.7 million in 1982 to \$7.8 million in 2018. That's an increase in income of \$5.1 million. In contrast, the average income of someone at the top 10 per cent level in 1982 went from \$125,000 to \$186,000, an increase of \$61,000. The top 10 per cent all received more over the thirty-six years, but the few at the very top saw increases on a scale that is hard to grasp.

How Much Tax Do Wealthy Canadians Pay?

Of course, incomes before tax are one thing, and incomes after tax are another. The higher your income, the more income tax you pay. Canadian income tax is "progressive," which means that the percentage taxpayers pay on the dollars they receive increases as the amount of money they receive grows.

In 2021, the highest combined tax rate on the last dollar of income someone receives was between 47 and 54 per cent, depending on their province of residence. Just after the Second World War, Canada's highest "marginal" tax rate — that is, the rate charged on the last dollar received — was 80 per cent.[1] Top marginal tax rates were cut in 1972, in 1982 and again in 1987, by which time the average combined top rate in Canada was closer to 45 per cent.[2] So not only were the richest among us seeing soaring incomes, but they were also paying a smaller proportion of these higher incomes in taxes.

This trend was not unique to Canada. By the time the financial crisis hit the world in 2008, several high-profile economists had already gathered data showing the growth of extreme income inequality. In Canada, economists Armine Yalnizyan[3] (in 2021 an Atkinson Fellow on the Future of Workers) and Mike Veall[4] (a professor at McMaster University) carefully documented rising income inequality and noted Canada's historically low marginal tax rates on income.

Public pressure resulted in some small changes to top marginal rates in most provinces after 2009, and both the NDP and the Liberals ran on increasing top marginal tax rates in the 2015 election. After winning a majority government, Justin Trudeau kept his promise and added a new federal tax bracket of 33 per cent on income over $200,000. When combined with provincial rates, this resulted in an average combined top marginal tax rate of around 50 per cent.

Sometimes people get nervous when we start to talk about marginal tax rates over 50 per cent, and critics have pushed back loudly against recent increases. Marginal tax rates are not easy to understand, and people sometimes confuse the top marginal rate with their average, or effective, tax rate. This is why you sometimes hear people say things like, "if I make any more money, it will bump me into a higher tax bracket, and I'll end up worse off." This can happen at the low end of the income spectrum, especially when rent is set at a certain percentage of your income and other income supports are also clawed back as employment income rises. For most of us, though, that isn't how marginal tax rates work.

Example: Marginal and effective tax rates using 2020 federal brackets

Tax bracket	Marginal tax rate	Sample taxable income		
		$100,100	$270,100	$3,892,000
Tax paid on first $48,535 of taxable income	15%	$7,280	$7,280	$7,280
Tax paid on taxable income between $48,535 and $97,069	20.5%	$9,949	$9,949	$9,949
Tax paid on taxable income between $97,069 and $150,473	26%	$788	$13,885	$13,885
Tax paid on taxable income between $150,473 and $214,368	29%		$18,530	$18,530
Tax paid on taxable income over $214,368	33%		$18,392	$1,213,619
Total tax paid		$18,018	$68,036	$1,263,263
Effective tax rate		18%	25%	32%

In the example table, you can see that someone whose taxable income is at $100,100 has a highest marginal tax rate of 26 per cent, but an average tax rate of only 18 per cent. Similarly, someone with a taxable income of $270,000 pays the highest marginal tax rate of 33 per cent on income over $214,368, but an average tax rate of only 25 per cent. Only when taxable income is much higher than the threshold for the top bracket does the marginal rate come close to the overall average rate.

This example assumes absolutely no tax planning or other deductions and so shows a much higher average rate than the rich in Canada actually pay. In the world of the one per cent, the gap between the marginal rate and the effective rate is quite significant compared to everyone else, thanks to the tactical skills of their financial planners and all the loopholes in our tax system. In fact, the effective tax rate for the top one per cent of families ranged from 4 per cent for those who paid the lowest tax rate to 28 per cent for the highest.

In spite of all the talk about a tax rate of 50 per cent, the best-off Canadians actually pay a far lower average rate. The data show that virtually no one pays 50 per cent of their income in taxes, no matter how much they earn. The average tax rate that families in the top one per cent actually paid was only 18.3 per cent in 2018,[5] according to data from Statistics Canada available in early 2021. The one per cent with incomes above $3,900,000 are paying income tax at exactly the same average rate of 18 per cent as someone with an income of $100,000.

How does this happen? Active "tax planning" includes donations to charities and political parties, compensation taken as stock options or dividends instead of income, shifting gains and losses between years and much, much more. Most of this work by accountants and lawyers on behalf of wealthy high-income recipients lowers the amount of their income that is considered taxable or shifts it into forms of income that are taxed at lower levels, like capital gains. All these activities constitute legal tax avoidance. Outright tax evasion is something else. The latter is illegal, though it still happens on a significant scale in Canada (see Chapter 7).

This situation is not unique to Canada. In the US, world-renowned tax experts Emmanuel Saez and Gabriel Zucman estimated that since the 1960s the effective tax rate paid by the top 0.1 per cent of tax filers has fallen from 60 per cent to less than 30 per cent. Saez and Peter Diamond — Nobel laureate in economics and one of the world's leading experts on public finance — have done extensive research on the issue of taxing the very rich and they have determined that the optimal tax rate for the highest-income earners would be 73 per cent.

Would Higher Taxes on Incomes Drive Rich Canadians to Leave?

A thorough analysis conducted by Lars Osberg, economics professor at Dalhousie University — former president of the Canadian Economics Association and expert in income inequality — also showed that Canadian governments could have successfully collected much more income tax from the country's top income recipients than they currently pay. He found that a combined top marginal tax rate of 65 per cent was consistent with historical averages in Canada and feasible to implement.[6] Such a change, he estimated, would yield between $15.8 and $19.3 billion for governments to use on public programs. It could, for instance, potentially cover the cost of eliminating all university tuition in Canada.[7]

The most common argument against higher rates of income tax on top income recipients is that high-income individuals would simply move to another country to avoid paying these rates. High-income lawyers, accountants, journalists and business people often make this case in angry articles in Canada's national newspapers, claiming that higher income taxes would be counterproductive and result in a "brain drain" to the US. Some will point to classic examples of Canadians who took their money and left the country — often for pleasant warmer spots in the Caribbean.

New Brunswick's K. C. Irving was among the first Canadian multimillionaires to leave the country to avoid taxes when he moved to Bermuda in 1971. He structured his fortune so that he paid no taxes in Canada on the profits he made from the Irving Oil company, the Irving forestry empire and the Irving newspaper chain, and his family could inherit it all tax-free.

How often has that happened? Is an increase in the top income tax rate likely to produce many more multi-millionaires and billionaires departing for the Caribbean? Osberg looked at international evidence and evidence from within the US and found that few wealthy individuals move countries to avoid taxes. He pointed out that this finding makes perfect sense if you consider the fact that even the wealthy benefit from the investments that governments make in high-quality public services.

A top income recipient acting rationally would be happy to pay more tax in the good years to ensure that they would have the services and support they might need in the bad years. By paying a somewhat higher tax rate in Canada than in some other countries, the rich have access to quality services like head-to-toe health care, high-quality education for their children and grandchildren and the safety and security that living in a more equal society brings. You can't only factor in the costs of higher taxes; you have to consider the benefits those taxes bring as well.

Someone looking for a new country with lower taxes has a surprisingly limited range of possibilities. Canada in 2021 was solidly in the middle of the pack for rich nations when it came to tax rates. Many countries — including Japan, France, Belgium and Sweden — have a much higher effective tax rate.[8] Japan, the third-largest economy in the world, has a marginal income tax rate of 55 per cent — 5 per cent higher than Canada's.[9]

Looking abroad, it becomes clear that the Canadian government has room to increase its level of taxation on the richest. Despite the loud claims, higher taxes at the top would not cause an exodus en masse or ruin the economy. Rather, it would result in observable and measurable benefits that would, for real this time, flow to everyone.

Would Anybody Actually Pay the Higher Tax Rate?

The other main argument against raising top marginal tax rates is that the rich have access to high-priced and highly skilled accountants and lawyers who will help them find ways to avoid paying these rates. Osberg examined this argument as well. There is evidence that the top 0.01 per cent would put lots of effort into taking advantage of tax avoidance and evasion opportunities. This only makes it more important to tax capital gains at a higher rate, close loopholes and increase overall enforcement alongside any increase in top marginal rates, as proposed by the NDP during the 2019 election campaign.

How Much Would a 2 per Cent Tax Increase on Top Income Recipients Bring In?

Along with these changes, the NDP proposed increasing the marginal tax rate for the one per cent from 33 to 35 per cent. This would result in an average combined federal and provincial top marginal tax rate of 52 per cent — well below the combined rate of 65 per cent considered by Lars Osberg and other economists. This modest 2 per cent increase would increase federal government revenue by about $900 million, according to an estimate by the independent Parliamentary Budget Officer.[10]

If we repeat the sample taxable incomes from our example table earlier in the chapter and compare the increases in taxes that individuals might experience from this change, we see clearly that this would impact the one per cent of income earners the most, and the impact would increase as income rises.

No one with taxable income under $214,368 would see any change. Someone with taxable income of $270,100 would see an increase of just over $1,000 on their total tax bill if the top marginal tax rate increased from 33 to 35 per cent. But someone in the top 0.01 per cent of income earners, earning $3,892,000 per year, would pay an additional $73,000 per year. That additional amount, paid by the small number of Canadians who would be affected by this tax increase, would add up to almost a billion dollars a year in additional revenue for governments.

Example: Difference between 33 and 35 per cent top marginal tax rate

		Sample Taxable Income	
		$270,100	$3,892,000
33% marginal tax rate	Tax paid on taxable income over $214,368	$18,392	$1,213,619
	Total tax paid	$68,036	$1,263,263
	Effective tax rate	25%	32%
35% marginal tax rate	Tax paid on taxable income over $214,368	$19,506	$1,287,171
	Total tax paid	$69,151	$1,336,816
	Effective tax rate	26%	34%
Difference in taxes paid		$1,115	$73,553

Conclusion

At a time when government deficits are running in the hundreds of billions of dollars, a single billion may not seem that much. As Lars Osberg and many other economists in Canada and around the world have pointed out, in the postpandemic era, governments will have to decide how to increase their revenues to pay for badly needed improvements in public health measures and social services. In a wealthy country, where the need for better public services exists alongside the need to reduce extremes of inequality, the obvious measure is to look to the richest among us to share their wealth.

A progressive, fair, and efficient tax system forms an essential part of a dynamic and just society. Increasing the top marginal tax rate, combined with the other measures proposed in this book, will help us to achieve this objective. As economist and Nobel Prize winner Joseph Stiglitz says, "It is only fair that those who have greater capacity to pay — and who typically gain more from our economy — contribute more."[11]

CHAPTER 7

TACKLING TAX HAVENS

Tax havens have received lots of attention in the media. Many Canadians have been called out publicly for using tax havens to hide their income and pay less tax. Yet the risks of public exposure and — probably worse — follow-up investigations by the Canada Revenue Agency seem to have had no effect. These devices continue to be used by the richest people and big corporations to "avoid" (legally) and "evade" (illegally) their taxes.

Despite public outrage and clear proposals by academics and advocates for reform and tax fairness, progress on shutting down tax havens is so slow and so paltry that it seems virtually nonexistent. Our governments' failure to act fuels public frustration, cynicism and political disengagement. At the end of the day, Canadians know that taking no effective steps to stop the use of tax havens means that the rest of us will have to pay more tax or make do with fewer public services, or both.

Canadians and citizens of other wealthy countries know a great deal more about the history and extent of tax havens than they used to, thanks to two massive leaks of documents from leading players in the worldwide tax haven business. The documents leaked to major international and Canadian news media were labelled the Panama Papers and later, the Paradise Papers. These two leaks identified wealthy individuals and large corporations around the world that used tax havens to avoid and evade tax. Many Canadians were on that list.

This chapter takes a deep dive and fills you in on one of the most unacceptable aspects of our legal system. Alain Deneault — a philosopher and one of the best experts in the fight against tax havens in Canada — calls it "legalized theft."

What Are Offshore Tax Havens?

As explained in Part One, some wealthy Canadian individuals and big corporations structure their businesses to have subsidiary companies they own and run located in countries large and small that have low tax rates. A Canadian-based company then transacts business with its foreign-based subsidiary in ways that lead to the foreign-based company recording profits instead of the Canadian company. Taxes on these profits are assessed in the foreign country rather than in Canada. Foreign countries that charge little or no tax on these profits are called "tax havens."

Of course, lots of big Canadian corporations have legitimate business activities in foreign countries and set up subsidiary companies they own to conduct that business there. What sets tax havens apart is that the subsidiaries set up in the tax haven conduct no legitimate business activity. Their only business is helping the parent Canadian corporation avoid tax.

Often a corporation using tax havens will establish a whole network of subsidiary companies in multiple tax havens. Once set up, the subsidiaries undertake complex transactions, buying and selling from one company to the other and lending and borrowing money back and forth, all with no purpose other than to earn profits in tax haven countries where little or no tax has to be paid.

And miracle of miracles, once a foreign subsidiary has earned big untaxed profits for its Canadian owners, those profits can be brought back to Canada without any additional tax being paid. Why? Because the Canadian government has a tax treaty with the tax haven that says Canada won't levy additional taxes on profits made in that country, in exchange for the tax haven not levying taxes on profits made in Canada by a genuine company from the tax haven country.

Offshore tax havens are included in what tax experts call "tax avoidance," which consists of domestic and international strategies to avoid tax through contravening the spirit — but not the letter — of the law. That's what Alain Deneault means by legalized theft.

Tax *avoidance* differs from tax *evasion*, which involves deliberate underreporting of payable tax by concealing income or assets and by making false statements. In other words, tax evasion is flat-out illegal. As Deneault explains,

> *While corporations [and wealthy individuals] clearly benefit from public services and the institutions of the common good (e.g. water supply systems, road construction and maintenance, educated labour force, legal security, government support programs that guarantee social peace, research and development grants, airport and shipping infrastructures, etc.), they are now able to scatter their assets, recording them in jurisdictions other than the ones that have enabled them to amass their wealth. This is precisely how they avoid paying society what they owe in the places they are registered, they can do anything they want.*[1]

What makes a foreign country a tax haven? A jurisdiction would be considered a tax haven when its tax rate on corporations is at, or very close to, zero. These jurisdictions also have ultra-permissive legal systems that are designed to neutralize the legal systems of other countries and secrecy that hides and benefits the owners of capital. Often, investors don't have to have any tangible physical business activity in the jurisdiction to benefit from the tax breaks offered.[2]

A tax haven can be easily identified by looking at the economic dynamics of the country. Alain Deneault gives the example of Barbados in his book *Legalizing Theft: A Short Guide to Tax Havens*:

> *Barbados, for instance, is on a par with the town of Kitchener, Ontario, in terms of demographics. But while Kitchener city officials are busy trying to create "the right climate for businesses to succeed" through the management of a "$110-million economic development investment fund," Barbados has attracted over $72 billion in "investments" by Canadian corporations — investments that bear no relation to any industrial or trade activity actually carried in Barbados.*[3]

It's difficult for officials looking for new investment in Kitchener to compete against a country that allows companies to operate without many legal constraints and to pay little or no taxes when they record a big profit.

Though tax havens have many common features, each one has its own particular niche. For instance, wealthy individuals and corporations use Switzerland for wealth management; Luxembourg is a bank haven for managing multinational corporations; the Cayman Islands are a regulatory haven for high-risk finance; and so on. Even Canada figures on the list of tax havens as a "legal and regulatory haven for mining and exploration companies."[4] As Toby Sanger, executive director of Canadians for Tax Fairness and an economist, says, there is a constellation, a whole universe of tax havens and low-tax jurisdictions from which the wealthiest and the biggest corporations can pick to avoid paying tax.[5]

How Did We Get Here?

Tax havens were specifically created and set up to do exactly what they are doing. Canadian and other governments have sometimes contributed to their creation and other times simply chosen to turn a blind eye.

Most tax havens were designed by financial institutions in the world's largest cities and countries during the twentieth century. They have been purposely set up to allow wealthy owners and investors advised by those financial institutions to avoid taxes and other obligations in their home country without having to put a foot in those tax haven "paradises."

Canada — through its relationship with British dependencies and former colonies in the Caribbean — has played a central role in the development of tax havens. Alain Deneault, in his book *Paradis fiscaux: la filière canadienne*, explains that a former governor of the Bank of Canada contributed to making Jamaica a tax haven, a former Canadian federal minister of finance developed the Bahamas' offshore regulations, and a former Conservative Party member helped structure the Cayman Islands' banking laws.[6] We are still paying the price of these actions.

Knowing that Canada is behind the establishment of several tax havens, you might guess that the Canadian government has not put laws and regulations in place to prevent Canadians and Canadian companies from taking advantage of them. And you'd be right. Canada has made it easier to use tax havens over time by signing tax treaties and agreements with many of these jurisdictions. These tax treaties facilitate moving funds from one jurisdiction to another and creating shell companies for the sole purpose of sheltering money from tax.[7]

As we noted in Chapter 1, globalization, free trade agreements and the desire to attract capital started a race between countries to entice big multinationals. Key strategies included lowering income tax rates and allowing and enabling the use of offshore tax havens. Canada has done both.

The federal government has lowered corporate taxes significantly, as we have noted, and has also signed numerous agreements with tax havens. Many of these treaties were ratified through Bill S-2, passed in 1980. At that time, NDP finance critic Bob Rae warned in a House of Commons speech that treaties like the one with Barbados would drastically cut the tax rate for Canadian companies operating abroad. History has proved him right.[8]

What's the Problem Now?

As the CBC reported in 2016:

> *Barbados, a tax haven, is the No. 3 destination for Canadian money going abroad. Corporations and wealthy Canadians have moved nearly $80 billion there — behind only the U.S. and U.K. as an investment destination. There's more Canadian money parked in Barbados than in France, Germany, Italy, Japan and Russia combined.*[9]

A big proportion of this parked money should actually be owed to the Canadian federal treasury and is money that we could use to invest in public services and infrastructure. And as noted by Alain Deneault,

> *These corporations benefit from public infrastructure. They use roads, they have access to water, to electricity.*

> *Their employees are trained by the state. They benefit from the social system. But they don't pay for it. They don't pay their fair share and they know how to manage it so they don't.*[10]

Concerns have long been raised and alarms sounded — by Bob Rae and the federal NDP, by the media reporting on the Panama Papers and the Paradise Papers, and by independent experts, including reports from Canada's Auditor General. Despite this, very little has been done by successive Liberal and Conservative governments to fix the use of offshore tax havens. Since 2009, Conservative and Liberal governments have both signed new treaties with many more tax havens. As explained in a 2017 investigation by the *Toronto Star* and *Corporate Knights* magazine, these tax treaties or Tax Information Exchange Agreements were promoted as a means "to prevent the double taxation of corporate profits, but in practice they make it possible for companies to avoid paying tax altogether, recording profits where there are low or no income taxes and then repatriating this income to Canada tax-free."[11]

These new signed treaties, along with the previous ones, have led to an exponential increase in the amount of money leaving Canada to be parked in tax havens. According to a 2020 report for Canadians for Tax Fairness, Canadian corporations had $381 billion in assets in 2019 in the top twelve tax havens, up by $10 billion from 2018 and representing an increase of 135 per cent in a decade.[12]

Which Canadian corporations are using tax havens to reduce the taxes they should be paying in Canada? Foremost among them are Canada's big banks, on whose boards the country's most distinguished and respected senior business leaders gather. The big banks in Canada all have subsidiaries in tax havens and avoid paying part of their taxes while making incredible profits and charging exorbitant fees to Canadians.

NDP. The report showed that after more than 450,000 international electronic money transfers worth "over $450 billion" between the 2016–17 and 2019–20 fiscal years were reviewed, no charges were laid against anyone involved. None. As NDP national revenue critic Matthew Green said, "Could there really have been none that broke the rules?"[23] This seems improbable.

Why no action from Canada on tax haven use, even with the information from these high-profile leaks? The Trudeau government increased funding for the Canada Revenue Agency's work on tax enforcement — after Stephen Harper cut it significantly — but Canada's tax laws pose the biggest barrier to blocking tax haven use. As tax expert Toby Sanger said in 2020, "[The Liberals] haven't done much so far. They're really doing the bare minimum when they could be a leader."[24] Recent changes to Canadian tax laws and treaties have made tax haven tactics easier and ultimately conferred legality on many practices. Until these laws are reformed, active tax avoidance remains nearly impossible to prosecute successfully.

The fate of a federal government case against Loblaws offers an instructive and revealing case study: The federal government accused the company of failing to comply with Canada's tax laws by shifting profits to a subsidiary "bank" that it had established in the tax haven of Barbados. The Canada Revenue Agency assessed Loblaws as owing an additional $368 million in unpaid taxes arising from the use of this Barbados tax haven subsidiary.

In April 2020, the Federal Court of Appeal sided with Loblaws, overturning an earlier conviction and finding that the law permitted Loblaws to do what it was doing. While the federal government appealed this case to the Supreme Court, the case showed how hard it is for the Canada Revenue Agency to fight the use of tax havens when the courts find that the law permits their use. The fact that the federal government lost $368 million in taxes from a single Canadian corporation in this single case

Solutions

Not all political parties have supported or turned a blind eye to this type of economic strategy pursued by large corporations and ultra-rich individuals. The NDP has consistently made cracking down on tax havens a priority. It's a clear issue of fairness, but also of resources that we could use to build a prosperous and equitable society and economy. It's a question of values, priorities and vision for the country.

In 2017, Murray Rankin — a lawyer and NDP member of parliament for Victoria — introduced Bill C-362 in the House of Commons. This legislation would deny tax breaks for transactions with no real "economic substance." If passed, it would ban the use of shell companies that serve no economic purpose other than to protect the wealth of the ultra-rich. It shifted the burden of proof, requiring companies to prove the "economic substance" of their offshore subsidiaries for them to be legitimate for tax purposes. Rankin explained the impact of this measure:

> *Right now, for example, corporations can put money in a Canada-based investment corporation, then legally create a subsidiary corporation in a tax haven, like the Cayman Islands, and transfer money into this shell corporation. And the big problem is that investment income is taxed in tax havens at either 0% or at a ridiculously low rate. Had that money remained in Canada, the corporation would have paid taxes on that income. As the law stands today, that corporation can then move this income back into Canada and avoid paying taxes on it. Does this sound like "tax fairness"? The current federal government apparently thinks so. And Starbucks may think so, when it uses tax havens to arrange its affairs to save corporate taxes; however the coffee shop owner across the street cannot.*[29]

When asked to prepare an independent estimate on how much these proposed measures would bring in new revenue to the government, the Parliamentary Budget Officer reported that it would be more than $2 billion a year.[30]

The NDP has proposed several other measures that would make a big dent in tax havens:

- Review all existing tax treaties to identify those that let companies declare profits in other countries and then repatriate them to Canada tax-free. In these cases, Canada should end the double taxation agreement with the tax haven, ensuring that big corporations and wealthy individuals pay taxes in Canada like everyone else.
- Impose stronger enforcement and harsher penalties to deter wealthy individuals and corporations from engaging in international tax evasion.
- Impose legislation to address the professional promoters of tax evasion schemes, including lawyers and accounting firms such as KPMG.
- Increase funding for the Canada Revenue Agency and prosecution service by $100 million a year for the next ten years to give these agencies the necessary resources to investigate and shut down sophisticated tax avoidance and evasion schemes.

The Parliamentary Budget Officer estimated that this last proposal, which was part of the NDP's 2019 federal election campaign commitments, would more than pay for itself, bringing an additional $413 million in the first year.[31] In early 2021, he estimated that each additional dollar spent in enforcing tax compliance by the federal government would bring back more than four dollars in additional tax revenues.[32]

Conclusion

Tax havens have absolutely no economic and social value for our country. They serve only to provide a huge tax break for wealthy individuals and corporations while the rest of us pay the price. Tax havens allow many of the largest corporations in the world, including large Canadian corporations, to pay little or no tax on their profits. They give an enormous advantage to big business over our local small businesses, at a time when local businesses are finding it harder and harder to keep their heads above water, especially in the wake of the pandemic. And tax havens mean that some of the wealthiest Canadians pay less tax than you do.

No politicians admit to liking tax havens in public. In fact, some Canadian finance ministers have claimed that they want to clamp down aggressively on the practices described in this chapter. During his time as finance minister, from 2015 to 2020, Bill Morneau often spoke out on this topic. "We don't want to wait for the next Panama Papers to tell us whether or not someone may be trying to hide their income from taxation," he said in 2017. In a speech to the Toronto Region Board of Trade, he pledged to close loopholes and shut down tax havens: "When people pay their taxes, they want to know their neighbour pays roughly the same taxes. Right now there are some loopholes in our system that means that that is not necessarily always the case."[33] As the wealthy owner of Canada's largest human resources company, Morneau Shepell, and the husband of Nancy McCain of the wealthy McCain family, Morneau had the background knowledge to tackle tax havens aggressively. Yet at the time of his resignation in mid-2020, there had been little sign of action.

His successor, Chrystia Freeland, knows the world of the ultra-rich from a different perspective. During her career as a financial journalist and a reporter at the annual Davos gathering of the world's economic and political elite, Freeland rubbed shoulders with many of the individuals who benefit most from the use of tax havens. She authored a book about the super-rich,

The Plutocrats, in which she warns about the dangers of excessive inequality. In the job of finance minister, Freeland has the opportunity to take concrete steps to address inequality in Canada. Meaningful action to end the use of tax havens by Canadian corporations and wealthy individuals was open to her as of early 2021. If history is any guide, however, Liberal finance ministers talk about clamping down on tax avoidance by the wealthiest, but fail to act on it. Freeland's first budget in April 2021 was no different than previous Liberal budgets. While she acknowledged there is a problem, she once again announced "consultations" when some of the reforms needed are clear and simple.

Certainly, closing the gaps will be laborious. It will require great strength of character and the will and ability to stand up to virtually universal hostility from the wealthiest and most powerful people in Canada. Our economic elite has had this tap open for a long time and will fiercely oppose changes by any means possible.

New laws are needed. Liberal and Conservative politicians who decide to back measures to require wealthy individuals to pay more tax will be faced with outraged friends and contributors. Once the laws are passed, long court cases will be fought. Judges will find themselves having to choose between the interests of the wealthiest people in Canada and the interests of the rest of us. It will take a broad consensus of Canadians that the wealth of our country needs to be more fairly shared to defy the resistance of many of our wealthiest citizens and their agents and advocates.

CHAPTER 8

INCREASING CORPORATE TAXES

Former NDP leader David Lewis railed against Pierre Trudeau's economic approach of tax cuts and direct grants for corporations in the 1972 election campaign. Lewis's campaign targeting Liberal policies favouring what he called "corporate welfare bums" helped the NDP win the balance of power, with a minority Liberal government that depended on its support to stay in office. The book Lewis released during the campaign, titled *Louder Voices: The Corporate Welfare Bums*, documented his case against lower taxes for big corporations. Lewis would likely be greatly disappointed that we continue to hear the rationale that handouts to corporations are the only way to create jobs, but also not surprised.

Since Lewis's book was published, both the official corporate tax rate and the effective rate have been cut, supposedly to spur corporate investment in our economy. This has happened not just in Canada but globally, with rich countries finding themselves in a race to the bottom of tax competitiveness. As we have already documented, those tax cuts did not "trickle down" in Canada — the money was not invested in the economy, and it didn't end up in workers' pockets through higher wages. The benefits mainly ended up in the hands of rich managers, owners and shareholders.

Corporate tax cuts have only increased economic inequality and negatively affected the quality of our infrastructure and public services by reducing government revenues. Increasing corporate taxes can generate needed new revenues for governments — and help reduce inequality. Here's the evidence.

The History

Since the 1980s, as we have mentioned, the corporate tax rate has been heavily cut by successive Liberal and Conservative governments. The federal corporate tax rate was at 36 per cent in 1980.[1] Conservative Prime Minister Brian Mulroney reduced it to 27 per cent in 1987 and 1988. Liberal Finance Minister Paul Martin lowered it from 27 to 21 per cent and Conservative Prime Minister Stephen Harper lowered it even further from 21 to 15 per cent.

As we have pointed out already, the *Toronto Star* has reported,

> *Sixty-five years ago, people and corporations contributed equal amounts of income tax to the Canadian government. Since then, the scales have tipped in the corporations' favour. Corporate taxes have been slashed and people have been forced to make up the difference.*[2]

As of 2021, the corporate tax provided only about 20 per cent of government revenues.

But, as we have seen in the chapter on tax havens, the problem does not end there. Corporations, especially the larger ones, are able to use techniques to lower their effective tax rate and pay even less tax. We find ourselves with the same problem that we see with individuals. The combined federal-provincial corporate tax rate was at 26.6 per cent between 2011 and 2016, but the effective tax rate actually paid was only 17.7 per cent. This 8.9 per cent gap resulted in a shortfall of $62.9 billion in corporate income taxes for the government.

This represents $62.9 billion in corporate revenues that could have been used by the government to pay for schools, roads and public services we all rely on. Instead, that money was added to corporations' bank accounts.[3] Meanwhile, the Trudeau government boasted on its website that Canada's average effective tax rate was the lowest in the G7 and well below the average of the OECD.[4] We are temporarily "winning" the race — to the bottom.

The justification for these loopholes and tax cuts for large corporations has been that they would stimulate the economy. Corporations were supposed to put those savings back into productive investments that would grow the economy and create jobs. It never happened. When we look at business investment as a percentage of GDP between 1998 and 2016, it's flat — each year, Canadian businesses invested the same small amount, about 5.5 per cent.[5] Canadians for Tax Fairness summarized the situation:

> *Rather than stimulate investment, corporate tax cuts led to record company profits and mega surpluses in corporate cash. The result? More monopolies and less competition — not the jobs and economic growth initially promised. We know these cuts aren't working and they're costing governments billions while exacerbating inequality.*[6]

As we showed in Chapter 1, the companies that succeed in reducing their tax rates the most are the big Canadian banks. The

Toronto Star and *Corporate Knights* estimated that the big five banks in the country were able to avoid paying $22.9 billion in taxes between 2011 and 2016. Toronto Dominion Canada Trust (TD) was the big winner, avoiding about $6.3 billion in taxes.[7]

The big banks in Canada pay the lowest effective tax rate in the biggest and richest countries that make up the G7 group, at only 16 per cent. The US rate is the closest to Canada's, at 20 per cent. Germany's banks are furthest from the low Canadian rate, at 51 per cent. Germany's banks are big, innovative and profitable just like Canadian banks — the most noticeable difference is they pay a lot more in taxes. Not only are Canadians getting milked with high banking fees, but those banks are not paying their fair share of taxes on all the money they make from us.

It's tempting to point the finger at these banks and big corporations, blaming them for doing everything in their power to reduce the amount of tax they pay. It's very important to remember that the laws, rules and exemptions used by the banks have been consciously designed by the federal government to produce these low rates.

The Problems

To summarize, the economic and social experiment carried out in the last four decades of tax reduction for large corporations has not worked. The experiment has not delivered the promised effects and has created its share of problems. Gabriel Zucman, a world-renowned economist at Stanford University, explains it unequivocally:

> *Some countries, including Canada, have attempted to dramatically cut taxes on the wealthy and let corporate tax avoidance prosper. The result of these "trickle down" policies which started in the 1980s is now clear: income and wealth have boomed for a tiny fraction of the population, but this has not benefited the rest of*

> *the population at all. We must learn the lessons from this big natural experiment. The main lesson is that to have broad-based growth, we need an equitable tax system, where big corporations and high-earners in the financial industry and elsewhere pay their fair share.*[8]

Despite all these experiences that speak for themselves and the number of renowned experts who have debunked the trickle-down theory, the Liberals and Conservatives continue to recite their 1980s tape — saying that corporate tax competitiveness is a good investment and will be good for the economy. On top of this, we see a return to the refrain of the 1970s: that targeted tax incentives (what some might call loopholes) help create jobs.

The lack of transparency and honesty on this subject is beginning to resemble the denial of the climate crisis by oil companies and their friends in politics. No matter what the data have been saying for decades, the same message continues to be hammered home: we must continue down that path, it's good for the economy. For an economy that only works for the rich, maybe so. For an economy that benefits the big oil companies to the detriment of the planet, perhaps. But our governments are elected to represent us, to work for us all, not for the privileged and influential minority. We pay taxes, we lose quality public services and this system continues to be justified by effects that no one observes.

Tax cuts for large corporations increase economic inequality, and they are not a good economic investment compared to many other spending alternatives. As economist Armine Yalnizyan has documented, corporate tax cuts are the least effective job creation measure.[9] Each dollar spent on a tax cut would yield only 20 cents in economic growth.[10] Compare this to early childhood education investments, where each dollar invested yields a six dollar return to the economy (as assessed by the

Conference Board of Canada).[11] There are many other measures that the government could have chosen that would have truly boosted our economy for everyone, but they have chosen to side with the wealthy here again, as on so many other occasions.

Liberals and Conservatives often claim that tax cuts for corporations will help workers and consumers, and that they will encourage competition between businesses. In fact, corporate tax cuts foster an increase in monopolies, putting more power into the hands of fewer companies. As we have seen in Chapter 1, monopoly and oligopoly foster the exploitation of both consumers and workers. Joseph Stiglitz, a Nobel laureate and professor at Columbia University, offers this analysis:

> *In Canada, the evidence is that increasingly a larger fraction of income to corporations is related to excessive profits. Lower tax rates encourage firms to engage in more excessive profit seeking. You have greater incentives to create more monopoly power, to lobby [the government], because you get to keep a larger fraction of the returns from the lobbying activity.*[12]

Liberals and Conservatives may also say to you that a low corporate tax rate will attract businesses to Canada — that if we keep our rate lower than everybody else, more investments will come. As we have seen, corporate investment has been flat for many years. Peter Nicholson, former Finance Canada deputy minister, concluded that "corporate behaviour is generally driven more by opportunity and competition than by tax rates per se . . . I don't think raising or lowering taxes has a hell of a lot of influence on where companies invest."[13]

Ultimately, when taxes are lowered for large corporations, they pay less regardless of whether they create or cut jobs.

Solutions

In the 2019 election campaign, the NDP proposed to return corporate taxation to the level it was in 2010 — 18 per cent instead of the current 15 per cent. In other words, the NDP proposed a reasonable increase that would still keep Canada's corporate tax rate in the same range as those of Japan, Australia, France, Germany and many other countries in the OECD.[14] During that same campaign, the Parliamentary Budget Officer estimated that doing so would bring $6.2 billion in additional revenue in the first year, progressively increasing to $8.3 billion in year nine.[15]

The Conservative government in the UK announced in March 2021 that corporate tax rates will be increased from 19 per cent to 25 per cent by April 2023. In the United States in spring 2021, the Biden administration set a course for reversing the wholly ineffective corporate tax cuts of the Trump era. US Treasury Secretary Janet Yellen even proposed a global minimum tax rate for large corporations.

Excess Corporate Profits During COVID-19

Throughout the COVID-19 crisis, most Canadians and small businesses owners in Canada struggled to get by. From staying employed and keeping a roof over their heads to keeping the lights on in their businesses, COVID-19 was devastating for the people and our economy. As Canadians struggled with too many of us living paycheque to paycheque, the very wealthiest among us got richer and some very lucky corporations made record profits because of the pandemic.

The COVID-19 crisis did not affect every person, nor every business, equally. While many small and medium-sized businesses barely kept their doors open, some large companies made record profits. The one that comes to mind first is Amazon. While the health crisis was raging, Amazon increased its revenues dramatically, all at the expense of the revenues of many local small- and medium-sized businesses that did not have the time or money to make a quick transition to online sales. Amazon's leap forward was achieved in part on the back of poor employee working conditions, loopholes and regulations that benefit the company, and unfettered exploitation of the planet.

If we look at the figures for the third quarter of 2020, Amazon tripled its profits and increased its earnings by 37 per cent compared to the previous year.[16] The company does not reveal its figures for Canada alone, but no doubt a significant portion of this growth came from here. To add injustice to inequity, Amazon does not pay corporate taxes in Canada. Yet this company benefits from Canadian consumers, workers and infrastructure, and it makes sky-high profits, cutting into the business of local small and medium businesses who had to close during the pandemic. We discuss taxation issues regarding the web giants in the next chapter, but you get the picture.

Amazon was not the only multinational company to have made record profits during the pandemic; Walmart and Costco were also in that special club. Some Canadian banks got a good ride and increased their profits in 2020. Another winner was Shopify, a Canadian multinational e-commerce corporation that offers online retailers a suite of digital services. COVID-19 made its already successful business explode. During the third quarter of 2020, Shopify increased its revenue by 96 per cent and its gross profit by 88 per cent compared to 2019,[17] making it a record quarter for the company. Those record profits helped Shopify's owner, Tobi Lutke, add an additional $6.6 billion to his wealth during the first months of the pandemic.

A Wartime-Style Excess Profits Tax

While Shopify was making its new revenues and profits through helping small businesses transition to e-commerce, many businesses across the country were struggling — or closing temporarily or permanently. How, then, can we justify such excess profits? And what happens in the post-COVID-19 recovery? Is it desirable that the giants of the world stand even taller after the pandemic? What about local businesses and buying local products? Working conditions? The fight against climate change? Recovering jobs that were lost?

Many economists in Canada proposed what is called an "excess profits tax" — a measure that was used in Canada and many other countries during both world wars to ensure that businesses that benefited from extra work and extra profits from the war effort did not end up with big profits at the end.

Canada taxed away up to 80 per cent of profits in excess of what was considered standard. These excess profits taxes often raised considerably more than the general corporate income tax. During the period 1941 to 1946, excess profits taxes in Canada generated \$2.2 billion, while the corporate income tax generated \$1.58 billion for the federal government.[18]

Tax experts consider that excess profits can be calculated as a company's profits either above its average for previous years or above a set percentage. For instance, during the Second World War, for large corporations the government averaged the profits of the three previous years. As an illustration, for one company this average could be 8 per cent and for another it could be 10 per cent. Any profit above this percentage was taxed at 75 per cent. The other model used determined a fixed percentage for all large companies, for example 7.5 per cent. Therefore, any profits above this percentage were taxed at a higher percentage such as 75 per cent.

US President Franklin D. Roosevelt described a tax on excessive profits as a measure to ensure that "a few do not gain from the sacrifices of the many."[19] Gabriel Zucman, a world-renowned economist and professor at the University of

California, Berkeley, is one of the strong proponents of such a measure in the US. He has described an excess profit tax as

> *a solution that has been used historically during periods of crisis. The idea is you have some corporation that disproportionately benefits from the crisis, either because their competitors are shut down or because they exploit the crisis by hiking prices.*[20]

Considering that the COVID-19 pandemic has been very much like a time of war and that many companies had to make great sacrifices while others enjoyed great benefits, federal NDP leader Jagmeet Singh proposed the idea of a tax on excessive profits to Justin Trudeau's Liberal government in the fall of 2020. This proposal is supported by history, by experts and by 68 per cent of Canadians, according to a poll by Abacus Data.[21] To implement this measure, Mr. Singh offered to work with the government and the Parliamentary Budget Officer to determine what form this tax should take for the specific circumstances of Canada in 2021.

The excess profits tax Jagmeet Singh proposed had three elements:

- The tax rate for excess profits should be above 50 per cent.
- Companies should be prevented from moving their headquarters overseas to avoid the tax.
- The tax should be temporary.

Despite the strong support of Canadians and the NDP's willingness to work with the Liberals, Justin Trudeau refused to adopt such a measure. In April 2021 the Parliamentary Budget Officer estimated that this measure would bring in roughly $8 billion in additional government revenues. This temporary revenue source would be extremely valuable to help fund federal measures for small businesses to recover and to help industries and Canadians out of work as a result of the pandemic.

CHAPTER 9

WEB GIANTS

As we all know, over the last few decades, technology has evolved at lightning speed, sometimes for better, sometimes for worse. It's evolving so fast that our laws and regulations no longer keep pace. The regulation gap creates significant repercussions that have major social impacts, including contributing to economic inequality.

The advent of digital platforms such as Netflix, Amazon, Google, Facebook, Spotify, etc. — the web giants — has led to serious problems regarding how states tax corporate profits. Their overly-rapid growth globally has led to a situation where they seem to be above the law, and it is very difficult to ensure that they are subject to the same rules as other companies. As well as increasing social and economic inequalities, these web giants and their near-monopoly on entertainment threatens the survival of our own Canadian artists, our journalists, our local businesses and our democracy.

In this chapter, we address the issues related to the fact that web giants are not subject to the same tax laws as other companies and the consequences of this situation. We offer solutions and explain why we think it is so important to act.

The Problem

The main problem with web giants is that they compete with local businesses, media and content creators on an uneven playing field. Most Canadian laws governing the broadcasting industry are decades old. The relatively new web giants are often not covered by these laws and regulations. Unfortunately, the same goes for our taxation system. As a result, at the time of writing in early 2021, web giants pay little or no tax on their revenues or profits in Canada. They don't have to collect sales taxes on the subscriptions they sell. And they are not subject to the same rules as their Canadian competitors in their respective industries.

The first problem concerns the taxes that are not paid. The digitalization of our economy allows these large companies to transfer their profits from countries where they get their sales to jurisdictions where the tax rate is low. They do exactly as we have seen with tax havens, but on a much larger scale. Canadian corporate tax laws were written on the premise that a company's profits would be taxed where the economic activity took place. This was put in place to prevent companies from being taxed several times on the same profit. The web giants have found ways around this premise.

Here's a concrete example: when a company produces goods in the US and sells them in Canada, the company pays taxes on its profits in the jurisdiction where it produces its goods, in this case the US. Of course, when these laws were written, digital platforms did not exist. When everything is digital, the web giants structure their businesses to "produce" their goods in whatever country taxes them the least on their profits. The result is that their level of taxation is reduced to almost zero.

A 2019 report by the Tax Mark Foundation showed that in the period 2010–19, the six web giants — Facebook, Apple, Amazon, Netflix, Google and Microsoft — avoided paying more than $100 billion in taxes worldwide. Amazon is the champion of this group: it paid only $3.4 billion in taxes globally while it made revenues of $960.5 billion.[1] That's a tax rate of 0.35 per cent. And as the Institute of Economic and Taxation Policy reported, Amazon paid zero federal taxes in the US in both 2017 and 2018 despite making $16.8 billion in profits in that country during those two years.[2] The situation is similar for all of the web giants.

Since these companies pay almost no taxes around the world and almost no taxes in the US, it is not surprising that they pay no taxes in Canada. This, to repeat, is despite making significant revenues in Canada. The Yale Report — a report commissioned by the federal government on broadcasting and telecommunications — recently documented that the web giants are steadily increasing their market share of the distribution of media content in Canada every year. Netflix is one of the biggest players in Canada, with estimated revenues of $1.6 billion in 2018. The Yale Report estimated that Apple's iTunes sold $330 million in audiovisual content in Canada in 2018.

Along with sales to consumers, the web giants earn enormous revenues from selling advertising. Facebook's estimated advertising revenues in Canada were $1.6 billion in 2017, while Google garnered an estimated $3.4 billion from advertising sales in the Canadian market in that same year.[3] Remember that all this income is generated from economic activity in Canada — but no taxes are paid. This is obviously a serious disadvantage for Canadian businesses that actually pay taxes in Canada.

The wealth generated by these web giants has found its way into the hands of very few tech founders: Elon Musk, Bill Gates, Mark Zuckerberg and Jeff Bezos among others. Their wealth is a product of the global dominance of the companies they started — but it is magnified by the fact that their companies pay so little tax. This distortion creates individuals and companies that are powerful enough to threaten states that attempt to change the rules. As a result, the rules remain in place, so that these companies can continue to dominate their markets.

As if all this wasn't enough, these web giants have not been required to collect sales taxes when they sell to Canadians, often giving them another 7 to 15 per cent advantage over Canadian companies. Although this tax is ultimately paid by the Canadian consumers, the fact that these foreign companies don't have the same obligation as Canadian companies adds to the unfairness of the system. Though the federal government announced its intention to address this issue in mid-2021, Canada lagged behind other countries and lost potential tax revenue as a result. In fact, in early 2021, Canada and the US were the only G7 countries that didn't require those web giants to collect sales tax. Many jurisdictions, including Quebec and Saskatchewan, had already moved on this issue.

The second problem concerns support for Canadian content. In the broadcasting environment, web giants like Netflix, Facebook and YouTube (owned by Google) do not have to contribute to Canadian content as Canadian broadcasters do. The rules governing Canadian broadcasters — including TV networks, specialty channels and cable companies — simply do not apply to the web giants. They have of course grown quickly, but Canadian industry experts have seen this coming for some time. Little changed in the years of their dramatic growth and as of early 2021, governments were still doing very little to address this problem.

Examining the difference between Netflix and Canadian broadcasters is instructive: The government rightly demands that broadcasters contribute to the creation of Canadian content by contributing to what is known as the Canada Media Fund. Among other things, this fund allows the creation of Canadian cultural content. In recent years, the fund financed the production of *Schitt's Creek* and *Murdoch Mysteries* — to name only two successful Canadian series. As Netflix took a greater share of Canadians' viewing time, we would have expected this web giant to contribute like other broadcasters. It did not, because the law did not include digital platforms. Otherwise, Netflix would have contributed almost

$480 million to Canadian culture in 2018. Its actual obligation was, well, $0. Not only goes this give Netflix an unfair advantage over its Canadian competitors, but it also weakens Canadian culture and reduces opportunities for our own artists and creators.

The third problem is the special treatment given spending on digital advertising on foreign advertising channels. A key loophole in Canadian tax law that favours the web giants to the detriment of their Canadian competitors is the tax deduction allowed for Canadian advertisers who purchase advertising on foreign digital platforms like Facebook and Google. Currently, the *Income Tax Act* (in section 19) prohibits Canadian advertisers from deducting their expenses on advertising in foreign traditional broadcast and print media — but fails to extend that prohibition to digital advertising. The result is that Facebook, Google and other foreign digital platforms are treated the same way as Canadian advertisers, and Ottawa loses $1.1 to $1.6 billion a year in corporate taxes that would otherwise be paid, according to Friends of Canadian Broadcasting.[4]

At the beginning, this law was introduced to help support the Canadian media industry by encouraging advertisers to spend their dollars in Canada; now it is helping to destroy that same industry. Knowing that our media depend heavily on advertising revenues, this loophole is a huge gift to Google and Facebook and the source of enormous harm to Canadian newspapers and broadcasters whose advertising revenues have drastically shrunk, resulting in job losses, shutdowns and far less news coverage.

Adding insult to this injury, the Trudeau government significantly increased the portion of government advertising spending that goes to Google and Facebook platforms. The total in 2018–19 hit a record $15.8 million on those platforms.[5] Facebook and Google are really efficient in advertising, largely as a result of the enormous amounts of data they have collected from virtually every internet user. There is no need to add to their market power in Canada by giving them an exemption to a law designed to sustain the Canadian media industry.

These three problems demonstrate that the government, by its actions and inactions, subsidizes and benefits American digital multinationals to the detriment of Canadian companies and workers. When those who have the power to level the playing field fail to do so, it becomes difficult to believe their claim that they champion Canadian workers, Canadian businesses, Canadian media and Canadian culture.

The Consequences

The uneven playing field benefits the digital giants and their owners who are already extremely well off. At the same time, many workers in Canada have lost their jobs. In part as a result of Facebook and Google's monopolization of the advertising market, Canada saw 189 community newspapers and thirty-six daily papers close between 2008 and 2018.[6] This led to 16,000 journalists losing their jobs — nearly one-third of all working journalists in the country.[7]

Of course, these numbers represent human dramas: experienced and skilled journalists suddenly out of work, families that have had to relocate and cities and regions that no longer have any source of reliable local news. More than that, the impact of the digital giants is a threat to our democracy. When credible journalistic sources dry up, unreliable and sometimes dangerous sources of information (or misinformation) fill the gap and undermine our democratic civil life, increasing the polarization and radicalization of our society.

The media industry is of course not the only one to have been affected by these web giants — the cab industry, the retail trade and the cultural milieu have all been affected by job losses and shutdowns of local businesses. Taxi drivers in many cities have lost their jobs or a significant portion of their income. Canadians for Tax Fairness has summarized the picture:

> *The impact is increasingly being felt across all sectors, including transportation, accommodation and retail as giants such as Amazon have shuttered many Mainstreet businesses. Uber was established as a digital platform so it can avoid tax on all different levels: sales taxes, payroll taxes and income taxes, despite the fact that its business completely relies on publicly funded roads and other infrastructure.*[8]

The result of these digital disruptors is that wealth is shifted from the middle class and workers to the few giants of the web, mostly in the US. And the longer our governments delay action, the more these giants increase and expand their market power. It is important to remember here what economist and Nobel laureate Joseph Stiglitz pointed out: market power gets translated into political power.

The web giants have become so powerful that they are now able to publicly threaten entire countries with backlash if legislators do not act as requested. This was evident in early 2021 when Google threatened to make its search engine unavailable in Australia if the government went ahead with its plan to make technology giants pay for content produced by news media. Their unfettered power was dramatically illustrated when Facebook cut off Australians' access to news as a bargaining ploy in its dispute with the Australian government — and shutting down vital news from public agencies about the pandemic and public health at the same time.

Other examples abound. When we talk about how sometimes corporations become more powerful than states, this is what we mean. Our governments have let web giants amass so much power that these companies and the individuals who own them feel entitled to determine how an entire society should be run. When we look at the continuing failure of governments to regulate or tax them, there can be no doubt about their enormous influence and power.

Another problematic consequence of the emergence of web giants is that they often seek growth at all costs. This leads to exploitation of workers, consumers and practices that are harmful to the environment. While Amazon was tripling its profits in 2020, the world's news media reported on workers who described the workplace as hell. "'Working conditions are hell': Amazon employees not surprised its warehouses have seen hundreds of COVID cases" said the headline in the *National Post* on December 23, 2020. The subhead went on: "'There is no social distancing, there is no sanitation,' said one worker. 'Many of them, 99 per cent of them, are scared of working there, but they have no choice.'"[9]

Our system and our governments allowed the web giants to pursue these business practices, to earn large untaxed profits and to become as powerful as they are. Governments allow them not to treat their workers humanely, respect the environment, or pay their fair share. Both Liberal and Conservative governments in Ottawa and in some provinces have given those companies a free ride. Blaming the giants allows governments to disassociate themselves from their responsibilities while the gap between the web giants and the rest of society continues to grow.

Solutions

There are many solutions to address the issues around the web giants, and they can be implemented by those who hold the key to this impasse — our governments. Around the world in early 2021 there were countries whose governments had the courage to address some of these problems. Australia, facing threats of retaliation from Google and Facebook, put in place a solution to address the crisis related to the reduction in Australian media's advertising revenues. Recognizing that a significant proportion of traffic on the Google and Facebook platforms is related to media content, the Australian government passed legislation to require those platforms to pay Aussie publishers for news content.[10]

France tackled the problem of taxing the revenues of web giants by introducing a 3 per cent levy on total revenues — not just profit

— from digital services earned in France by companies with revenues of more than €25 million in France and €750 million worldwide.[11] This tax is estimated to least generate €400 million (roughly $620 million CAD) annually. After the US government responded with threats directed at the French government, France agreed to assess the progress of negotiations at the OECD to find a solution to taxing the web giants. But when it declared itself unsatisfied with the progress of these discussions, France decided to move forward by starting to collect this new tax in December 2020.

As already mentioned, many countries and jurisdictions are requiring that the web giants collect consumer sales taxes (in Canada the GST/HST) on their sales. During the 2019 election campaign, the NDP pledged to force the web giants to collect GST/HST on the products they sell in Canada. Such a measure would generate $805 million in additional revenues in 2021–22, growing progressively to $1.26 billion in 2028–29, according to the Parliamentary Budget Officer.[12]

After years of opposing this approach, the federal Liberal government finally acknowledged the problem, and in its 2020 fall fiscal update, it committed itself to taking action. While the NDP fought and campaigned on this measure, the fact that the Liberals planned to start closing loopholes for the web giants with a measure that will make Canadian consumers pay rather than forcing the web giants to start paying taxes revealed the government's priorities.

For many years, the NDP fought for web giants to pay taxes on their profits like all Canadian companies. But after France brought in a tax on revenues rather than profits to prevent web giants from using loopholes to reduce the taxes they pay, the NDP proposed to use the same measure as France. Applied to Canada, a 3 per cent tax on web giants' sales in Canada — not their profits — would be applied to all corporations that have worldwide revenues of at least $1 billion and Canadian revenues of at least

$40 million. The Parliamentary Budget Officer estimated that this measure would generate $600 million in 2021–22, rising to $1.2 billion in 2028–29.

In the 2019 election campaign, after four years in power using delay tactics to avoid action, the Liberals promised to adopt this measure. After another few months in power, however, the Liberal government announced that it would wait to see if the negotiations with the OECD would conclude by January 2022 before moving forward with the three per cent tax — once again buying time for its friends in Silicon Valley, and probably bowing to pressure from the American government that had also been applied, unsuccessfully, to France.

A third measure that would address the problems caused by the web giants would be closing the loophole for money spent on digital advertising that goes outside Canada. The NDP promised in the 2019 campaign to close this loophole in the *Income Tax Act*. This measure would bring $1.1 billion in 2021–22, gradually increasing to $1.5 billion in 2028–29, according to the Parliamentary Budget Officer. The NDP also proposed that all web giants, regardless of their industry, would be required to follow the same rules as their Canadian counterparts.

There is no lack of solutions — only a lack of political will and political courage. Doing the right thing by tackling laws and policies that benefit only the ultra-rich web giants would bring in more than $2.5 billion per year in federal government revenues. Leaving that money with the web giants gets us nothing and costs us a lot economically and socially.

PART THREE: BUILDING SHARED WEALTH

Much of the attention focused on economic inequality in Canada broadly speaking has been on *income* inequality, while the role of *wealth* inequality has slid under the radar. The two phenomena are linked, and an understanding of one can help us reflect on the nature of the other.

Wealth inequality shows the opportunity that some groups have had to accumulate substantial resources over time. An understanding of wealth inequality shows us that economic inequality writ large is not random; rather, it's part of a self-perpetuating cycle. If economic inequality were based on pure chance, we would not see the extreme concentration of wealth and privilege that we have today in a small group of bankers, family heirs, CEOs and media barons.

As discussed in Part One, wealth accumulation in Canada has been fostered and facilitated by political decisions:

- To start with, corporate and personal *tax cuts* have allowed the wealthy to accumulate more wealth — and along with that of course, more power.
- This power has been used in turn to pressure governments to *deregulate* — especially by reducing protections for workers, consumers and the environment.

Quite simply, for decades we were told that the path to prosperity involved getting government out of the way and letting businesses do their thing. As we have seen, however, the decades-long global experiment with the trickle-down approach has conclusively shown that tax cuts and privatization do *not* fuel economic growth. But they definitely do help the rich get richer, creating more inequality in our society.

So, what do we do now? We need to do more than just tax wealth — we need to also change the built-in levers in our system that ensure the rich get richer and the poor stay poor. We'll need to look after one another better. This means levelling up by:

- Ensuring a basic standard of living through universal public services.
- Increasing workers' power, wages, and working conditions.
- Dismantling racism and other forms of oppression.
- Tackling the ultimate existential crisis — climate change.

Part Two of this book showed how it is possible to tax the rich and address both income and wealth inequality, specifically:

- An *annual net wealth tax* offers a good start toward a fairer economy, but is not enough on its own.
- *Changing how we tax capital gains* will raise almost as much money as a modest wealth tax.
- *Increasing the tax rate for corporations, closing loopholes, and increasing taxes on the highest income earners* will make the economy more equal, and raise revenue that can be used to fund important public investments.

Furthermore, we have seen how these proposed tax changes are well within the range governments in Canada have set in recent history.

In this part, we situate the discussion within the current economic context and suggest an updated view of government's role in creating wealth. We explore what could be possible if we invested the tax revenue proposed in Part Two and focused on building broad-based wealth in our communities. We contrast that with the alternative of doing nothing. Finally, we lay out the nature of the struggle that is before us.

CHAPTER 10

THE GOVERNMENT ROLE IN CREATING WEALTH

In its November 2020 Fall Economic Statement, the federal government projected that its program expenses for the 2020–21 fiscal year would total $620 billion, nearly $300 billion more than what it spent in the 2019–20 fiscal year.[1] The government also announced its plan for stimulus spending of between $70 to $100 billion, spread over the next three years, starting in 2021–22.

These are very, very large numbers. Such an increase in debt concerns many Canadians, especially anyone who lived through the 1990s public debt panic. But there are several reasons why the lessons that many drew from the 1990s do not apply to the post-COVID-19 world.

First, our current level of debt is lower as a proportion of the whole economy than it was in the nineties. The ratio of debt to GDP is a common way to compare the amount of public debt to the size of a country's economy. The 2020 Fall Economic Statement estimated that Canada's debt-to-GDP ratio will be just over 50 per cent for the next few years — well below the 1990s levels of 70 per cent.

Second, we have learned from international experience that there is no specific level of public debt that hampers economic growth or creates an economic crisis. What matters more for public debt sustainability is the cost of borrowing — how much the government spends every year to cover interest payments on its debt. Canada's cost of borrowing as a proportion of the total economy fell in 2020 — partly because interest rates fell and partly because the federal government shifted to longer-term borrowing, which carries lower rates. The cost of carrying federal debt was at an all-time high in the early 1990s, at over 6 per cent of GDP, but in 2021 it had fallen to 1 per cent of GDP and appeared likely to stay in that range for some time.

Third, the Bank of Canada's perspective on the balance between inflation and unemployment has changed since the 1990s. Years of wage stagnation and weak job growth have led our central bank to put more weight on supporting full employment. Rather than pressuring governments to hold back on stimulus, central banks around the world urged governments during the pandemic to use their capacity to borrow money to support their economies — even though that meant running deficits. The Bank of Canada, as well as other central banks, took dramatic action to buy up government bonds during the 2020 pandemic, ensuring governments had access to the money they needed to keep their economies afloat and the banks kept interest rates low. They signalled in 2020–21 that they would continue on this path until at least 2023, ensuring that governments could affordably spend and run deficits to fund economic recovery in the early 2020s.

We have also learned from the world's 2008–09 financial crisis. Canada's response to the financial crisis was much better than it might have been otherwise because the minority parliament pressured Prime Minister Stephen Harper and his team of fiscal conservatives to respond with appropriate stimulus spending. Shortly after the Conservatives won a minority government in the October 2008 election, Finance Minister Jim Flaherty presented a fall economic update that promised no stimulus and balanced budgets for the next five years. He did this even though Canada was officially in a recession as of October that year and unemployment rates outside the oil-producing provinces had begun to spike. The attempt by the opposition parties in Ottawa to oust Harper by forming a coalition failed, but they still forced Harper's government to offer a temporary two-year stimulus package in its January 2009 federal budget.

The stimulus package failed to address the underlying issues that had caused the financial crisis. Globally, leaders bailed out large manufacturers and banks that were "too big to fail," and left the rest of us holding the bill. The Occupy movement began to identify some of our system's flaws that had spurred economic inequality and social instability, articulating them in a way that resonated with a broad audience. Its analysis was dismissed by editorial pages as confused and ineffective, but Occupy and the follow-up work of academics and activists played a big role in getting most of us — the 99 per cent — to rethink how the economy should work.

We must continue to shift our understanding of how the economy and government work, so we don't repeat the approach to the 2008–09 financial crisis, with stimulus spending that simply props up the current system. After COVID-19, there's an opportunity to rebuild a new system that works even better. Canada can afford the increased debt of responding to the public health crisis; Canadians *can't* afford to keep heading down the road of tax cuts and growing economic inequality.

Going Beyond Redistribution

Government's role in addressing economic inequality is often described as providing a safety net — redistributing a minimum floor of resources to those who are not successful in the free market. These resources are usually provided as a mix of income supports and basic services — like subsidized child care and affordable housing. Most Canadians recognize that decades of tax cuts starved both income supports and basic services, at the same time that they enriched a lucky few.

The social safety net is only part of what government does. Its role in fostering an equitable economy goes beyond taxation and redistribution. Government is responsible for making sure the rules of the game are fair and fairly enforced so that everyone gets a more equal share of the wealth that they helped to create. But governments can also shape the economy's direction, by taking the long view and investing in public research and by creating healthy, sustainable markets.

Mariana Mazzucato, a professor in Economics of Innovation and Public Value at University College London, has done groundbreaking research on this role of government. She has uncovered the way that public investment in research and development has driven many of today's so-called private sector innovations. Her landmark book *The Entrepreneurial State* argued that *governments* are the big risk-takers in our economies and the private sector only takes on risk at the very late stages of product development.

Professor Mazzucato lays out how the key innovations behind Apple's iPhone — hard drives, touch screens, lithium-ion batteries and even Siri — all came from publicly funded research. Even Google's search algorithm was developed with public funding. Years of research from academics and other publicly funded researchers shaped most of the digital and communications advances that we enjoy today. Yet, as we have already seen, these very companies pay low effective tax rates globally, thanks to their use of tax havens and other tax avoidance schemes.

Mazzucato's analysis does not just conclude that wealth is socially created and that taxes are the price that profitable corporations should pay back to the public for our shared role in making their success possible. She explains why the narrative we have been telling ourselves — that the private sector is innovative while the public sector is bloated and lazy — isn't just wrong but counterproductive. Successful businesses, she points out, rely on the stream of innovations that come from publicly funded research and the market creation that comes from the public sector. In their absence, the private sector is not able to take on long-term and large-scale risk and will instead turn to other less productive ways to socialize risk and privatize rewards.

We have seen this in Canada with the privatization of crown corporations and other public services and the use of public-private partnerships (P3s) to build public infrastructure. Canadian journalist and author Linda McQuaig described this practice in her 2019 book *The Sport and Prey of Capitalists — How the Rich Are Stealing Canada's Public Wealth.*

In the 1980s and 1990s, governments across Canada sold off publicly owned corporations spanning a wide swath of sectors that involve essential infrastructure, including telecommunications, energy and transportation. As a result, profit became the overriding priority for these now privately owned companies, not quality or universality of access. The few remaining public enterprises, like SaskTel, Manitoba Hydro, Hydro-Québec and Alberta's public bank (ATB Financial) offer residents higher quality services than the private sector companies operating in the same industries and they do so at a lower cost to the public. Even so, SaskTel and Manitoba Hydro have been targets of Conservative governments looking to shrink them and set them up to be privatized.

McQuaig's account of the history of Connaught Labs[2] offers a particularly compelling example, in light of Canada's realization that the country no longer had capacity to manufacture the early breakthrough COVID-19 vaccines. The University of Toronto's Connaught Labs contributed to the discovery of insulin, as well as cutting-edge vaccine research for polio and smallpox, among other medical treatments. Connaught didn't just do cutting-edge research, but it also manufactured medicines and vaccines and sold them to provincial governments — at cost.

Because it was a public lab, Connaught could focus research on riskier problems — ones that were important, but not necessarily profitable. While Connaught had only a small share of Canada's overall pharmaceutical market, in its heyday in the late 1960s it was responsible for a much larger share — about 20 per cent — of the R&D[3] conducted by the industry in Canada. Researchers at Connaught partnered with other academics and institutions, magnifying the impact of their work.

The Brian Mulroney Conservative government privatized Connaught in 1985. Its owner in 2021 was a French multinational, Sanofi Pasteur. While the facility continued to manufacture vaccines, the level and focus of its R&D work declined dramatically. A publicly owned lab might have been able to adapt its focus to quickly work on manufacturing COVID-19 vaccines, but selling Connaught put an end to that possibility.

The story of an inefficient public sector and a job-creating private sector is told and retold — by the wealthy to justify their wealth, by lobbyists to bolster their demands for more tax breaks, and by newspaper editorials to explain why it does not make sense to tax the rich.

The real story about how the economy works needs to be front and centre in the fight to create a more equal and prosperous society. Of course, corporations and the wealthy should pay more taxes. Their wealth is dependent on our labour, combined with robust public infrastructure. But governments should also be clearer and more confident about the positive role they can play in creating future prosperity.

CHAPTER 11

WHAT WE COULD BUILD, AND HOW WE CAN ADDRESS INEQUALITY

The year 2020 showed that many of the programs that are supposed to help Canadians in times of need are simply not reliable. Years of underfunding and privatization in long-term care, failing infrastructure in schools and the lack of affordable child care for families — all resulting from decades of Liberal and Conservative cuts and privatization — have left us vulnerable. As we've seen, the wealthy have benefited hugely from the tax cuts that created these problems. There is no better time and no better reason to restore taxes on the wealthy than to fix these programs so that they will work well for all Canadians.

When we add up the tax measures that we have included in this book and add in some other small measures proposed by the NDP during the last election campaign — such as a 12 per cent luxury tax on aircraft, boats and vehicles over $100,000 and elimination of fossil fuel subsidies — we reach a conservative estimate of an additional $130 billion in revenue over four years, or just over $32 billion per year.

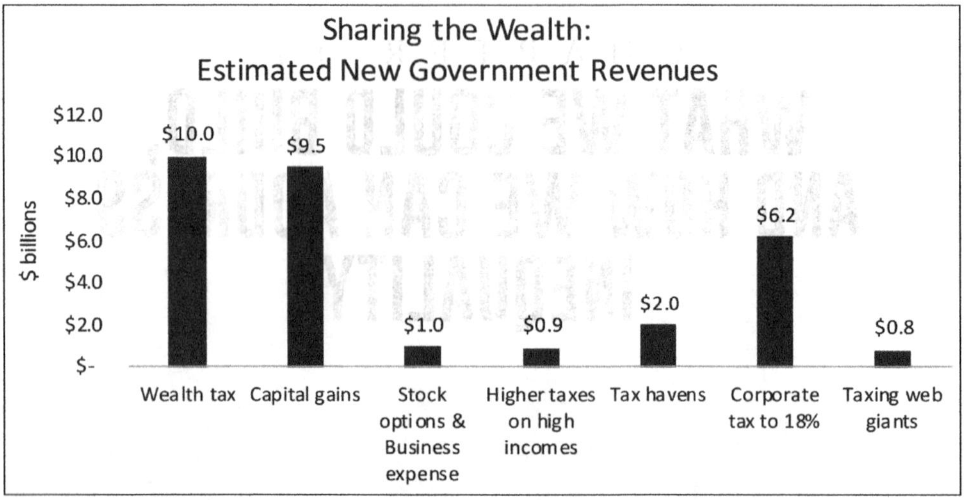

For context, the total federal budget in 2019 was $330 billion and Canada's entire economy was around $2 trillion. The level of taxation we have proposed would bring us closer to the range that we experienced before the big tax cuts of the 2000s.

An additional $32 billion is certainly a lot of money, especially for those of us who are not billionaires, but it's well within historical norms for Canada. And there is definitely room for going further in taxing big corporations and wealthy Canadians. In its 2020 Alternative Federal Budget,[1] written before the COVID-19 pandemic, the Canadian Centre for Policy Alternatives proposed tax fairness measures that would bring in $56 billion in additional tax revenue every year.

In February 2021, Canadians for Tax Fairness released a Fair Tax Recovery Plan that it estimated would raise an additional $70 billion in annual revenue for the federal government. The impact on the one per cent of paying an additional $70 billion? It would reduce their total ultra-wealth from $3 trillion to $2.93 trillion.[2] Though these 159,300 families would pay a little more, they would remain rich.

Visualizing alternate possibilities for our society becomes an important exercise in the effort to think beyond the imposed frameworks and structures we currently experience. We need to:

- Focus on investments that put people first.
- Address historic imbalances that prevented some communities from being able to accumulate resources in the first place.

Several key investments would augment the shift toward greater equality initiated by our tax fairness approach outlined above. To start, investing in all types of care work would help reshape gendered inequality. Care work is too often undervalued and underpaid. It is dominated by women, many racialized, with increasing numbers of migrant workers on temporary work permits. We need to invest in care work across the spectrum — from child care to elder care, from personal support workers to the physical spaces where they do their work. We also need to establish new democratic economic institutions to ensure that wealth remains in the communities that create it.

Child Care

One of the best investments Canada could make would be a national child care plan. Quebec's experience demonstrates that such a program pays for itself through the economic spinoffs it generates. For each dollar invested, it is estimated that the government has recovered $1.50 from the increased labour force participation of women.

A recent report from economist Jim Stanford at the Centre for Future Work found that such a program would create more than 200,000 new jobs and another 80,000 indirect new jobs, including 8,000 construction jobs needed to build or retrofit child care facilities. We estimate that this undertaking would cost at least $30 billion in the period 2021-26. It would generate between $17 and $29 billion in annual government revenues.[3]

Child care was expensive and hard to find even before the COVID-19 pandemic. It represents the second biggest expense for parents after housing and, in some cases, child care can actually cost more than a mortgage. The average cost of child care in Canada is $10,000 a year per child, with costs in some places like Toronto hitting as high as $20,000. Note that these statistics only apply when there is availability. In fact, 75 per cent of the country's children under age six do not have a place in licensed child care, forcing their parents to send them to unlicensed child care or stay home.

Between the beginning of the pandemic in March 2020 and February 2021, 100,000 women left the workforce — ten times more than men. As of February 2021, a total of 500,000 women who lost their jobs during the pandemic were still unemployed; most of these were low-income women.[4] In their April 2021 Budget, after being pushed by child care activists, the labour movement, and progressive economists, the Liberals came to the conclusion that they need to build such a program. Hopefully, this time it won't take another 20 years before seeing the light of day. Creating an affordable, public child care program is essential to a successful and equitable economic recovery in Canada. When women succeed, our economy prospers. A child care program would be a life-changing program for many parents and the beauty of it is that we would all see the benefits.

Health Care

When medicare was first put in place, it was meant to be the first stage of a system that would gradually be expanded to cover dental and vision, as well as other types of care, such as home care, long-term care and drug coverage. This never happened.

Federal funding was introduced for universal hospital insurance in 1957 and extended to cover physician visits in 1966. At that time, the federal government shared costs fifty-fifty with the provinces. The funding formula shifted over time, with increases often being tied to growth in the population and/or the economy. In his 2002 report of the Commission on the Future of Health Care, former Saskatchewan Premier Roy Romanow highlighted the significant gap between economic and population growth on the one hand and the growth of legitimate health care costs on the other. This gap meant that the federal government contributed a smaller and smaller share to health care costs over time, reaching a low of only 10 per cent in the late 1990s.

The 2004 Health Accord offered significant increases in federal funding, including a 6 per cent annual increase for ten years. These increases returned the federal funding share to 23 per cent of total costs by 2017. Unfortunately, Justin Trudeau implemented Stephen Harper's planned reduction in the growth of health care transfers back to only 3 per cent per year, amounting to a reduction of $31 billion over ten years.

Federal funding shortfalls have not been the only strain on the system — provinces also faced price pressures from the increasing cost of medicines and an aging population. The combination of underfunding and cost pressures have led to significant gaps in our health care system. Also, coverage for some essential services — such as dental care, drug coverage and mental health — remains almost entirely restricted to those with private insurance.

Long-Term Care

In the first wave of the pandemic, long-term care residents and staff accounted for 80 per cent of all COVID-19-related deaths in Canada, among the worst outcomes in wealthy nations. As of 2020, Canada spent 1.3 per cent of its GDP on long-term care — well below the OECD average of 1.7 per cent and in stark contrast with countries like the Netherlands (3.7 per cent), Belgium (2.1 per cent), France (1.9 per cent) and Japan (1.8 per cent).[5]

We have a mix of private for-profit, not-for-profit and publicly run long-term care homes and the outcomes from COVID-19 outbreaks were worst in the private for-profit homes. This was largely because of longstanding issues, such as poor enforcement of existing standards and a labour model that relies on too few badly paid precarious workers.

There are growing calls from seniors' advocates and unions to make long-term care an accessible, publicly funded and universal health care service. To do this, we need to:

- Significantly increase the number of public long-term care beds and staff.
- Ensure access and quality of care.

From the $130 billion of the new revenue generated by our proposed tax measures, we could invest an additional $5 billion in long-term care systems across the country. In addition to allowing the establishment and enforcement of national care standards, this funding would create numerous jobs and improve the quality of care for residents.

Dental Care

Oral health is one of the most unequal components of health care in Canada — most dental care isn't covered by public insurance plans. Those with the highest levels of oral health problems are also those with the greatest difficulty accessing oral health care, because of cost. More than one in five Canadians avoid the dentist every year because of the cost; consequently, emergency room visits due to dental emergencies cost taxpayers at least $155 million annually.

In the 2019 federal election, the NDP proposed a first step to universal dental care — providing insurance to those with a total household income below $90,000. The Parliamentary Budget Officer (PBO) estimated that this type of targeted program would help 6.5 million Canadians and would save households at least $1,200 annually. On average, this plan would cost $1.5 billion per year, but because so many without insurance (normally) simply go without dental care, the PBO predicted that costs would be double that in the first year of the program.[6]

Ultimately, we believe that dental care should be available to everyone as part of our health care system, but this program represents a critical first step to ensure that Canadians prevented from going to the dentist because of cost could now afford to go.

Pharmacare and Public Drug Research

Canadians consistently pay among the highest prices in the world for prescription drugs, as a result of our fragmented patchwork of drug coverage.[7] Not only do one in ten people in Canada go without medicine because they can't afford it, but every year almost one million Canadians cut back on other necessities to pay for their medication; another million Canadians have to borrow money to pay for it.

Preventative care improves health outcomes and saves money, but when patients can't afford their prescription drugs, they're more likely to need other interventions from the health care system. In 2016, about 303,000 Canadians had additional doctor visits, about 93,000 sought care in the emergency department and about 26,000 were admitted to hospital after being forced to forgo prescription medication because of cost.[8] HealthCareCAN, the national voice of health care organizations and hospitals across Canada, estimates that between 5.4 and 6.5 per cent of hospital admissions in Canada result from cost-related nonadherence to prescription medication, resulting in costs of approximately $1.6 billion per year.[9]

We estimate that it would cost about $10 billion annually to put a national pharmacare system in place. Once implemented, the pharmacare plan would be free for Canadians. Such a plan would:

- Shorten wait times.
- Free up more hospital beds for those who need them.
- Save provincial and territorial governments more than $4.2 billion per year.
- Save families more than $500 a year on average, whether they have insurance or not.
- Save employers $600 a year per insured worker.

We could go further and create a publicly owned company, a crown corporation, to research and manufacture vaccines and other critical medicines for Canadians. Such an investment would support high-quality public research and help us through future health crises. Restoring our capacity for public pharma research and manufacturing by creating a crown corporation is an example of the kind of actions government can take to shift the ways wealth is created and used. This would require startup investment, but publicly owned Connaught Labs was able to sell its medicines to provincial governments at cost and still break even, so eventually this investment is expected to be cost-neutral.

Climate Action

Despite increasingly urgent warnings from scientists about the threat posed by global warming, the federal government has moved slowly on necessary action, missed its targets and continued to spend billions of dollars on corporate subsidies in the oil and gas sector.

In his 2018 book *Getting to Zero*, long time Canadian social and environmental activist Tony Clarke outlined the need for massive public investments in three key areas:

- Renewable energy
- Public transit
- Building retrofits

Tony Clarke's activism included a key role in the Green Economy Network (GEN), and these three areas form the foundation of the GEN's campaign for "One Million Climate Jobs." Tony and GEN estimated that a total investment of $81 billion over five years from all three levels of government would be needed to meet Canada's climate targets.

While this seemed like a very large amount of money in 2018, spending on the pandemic provided some perspective on the capacity of the Canadian government to invest in high-priority and urgent measures. Some of this money has already been earmarked, especially in public transit, but too much of the funding in current plans relies on private sector involvement. Mariana Mazzucato is one of numerous economists who have warned that government reluctance to invest in necessary public climate infrastructure will delay effective climate action and increase the final bill.[10]

Supporting Democratic Economic Institutions and Climate Action

Harper's Conservative government pushed privatization through a crown corporation, Public-Private Partnerships Canada (PPP Canada). Using this vehicle, the government transferred infrastructure money to other levels of government, making it contingent on considering a PPP approach. In the 2015 election, Trudeau's Liberals promised they would transform PPP Canada into a *public* infrastructure bank, but once elected they changed their minds. The federal government's Canada Infrastructure Bank (CIB), established by the Liberals in 2017, was still mandated to support the development of public-private partnerships (P3s).

The federal Liberals committed $35 billion to CIB, an organization created to invest in infrastructure projects across the country but required to focus on projects that involve partnering with private investors — projects that would necessarily be designed to earn steady profits for big investors.

The story: Plenty of investor money was available, just waiting for profitable projects; the only thing needed was patient seed money from government to reduce the risk and attract investors.

The problem: Most big investments with steady revenue sources are, and should remain, public.

The result: CIB found little appetite among investors or the Canadian public for P3 transit projects or P3 water and wastewater treatment plants.

The case of the Canada Infrastructure Bank perfectly illustrates how much details matter and how what could be real change ends up being same old same old. While it shed the P3 language in its name and rhetoric, the fundamental principles underlying the bank's mandate and operations did not change. Liberals and Conservatives might tell you that this example shows there is no alternative, but they'd be wrong.

A *real* public infrastructure bank could:

- Invest in the low-carbon economy.
- Accelerate the adoption of clean technology.
- Create good jobs.
- Support local economic development.

Rather than aiming to profit rich investors, the priority would be fighting climate change and furthering community interests. The climate bank could invest in more green energy projects like those of the City of St-Hyacinthe in Quebec.

With its public bio-methanation plant, the city collects food waste from twenty-five municipalities and transforms it into natural gas. It uses this energy for its buildings and for the city's vehicles and in early 2021 was even selling its gas to local businesses. With this project, the city was increasing its revenues by $5.8 million, reducing the waste management problem of other municipalities, reducing greenhouse gas emissions by 49,000 tonnes per year and creating jobs for today and tomorrow. Projects like these can happen anywhere in the country. A public climate-focused bank could get more of them up and running faster.

The New Deal in the US was financed by a public infrastructure bank, called the Reconstruction Finance Corporation (RFC). RFC raised capital by selling bonds and lent the money to build key economic infrastructure. The infrastructure served its purpose in revitalizing local economies — allowing governments to raise enough tax revenues to repay the loans.

Public infrastructure banks can work well to mobilize large-scale resources for projects that would otherwise have difficulty accessing affordable financing. Just like the Canada Infrastructure Bank, their initial capital comes from government and their operations are backed by government guarantees, which allows these banks to raise money by selling low-cost bonds in financial markets. The banks can then provide long-term, low-cost loans to public entities like municipalities. This allows municipalities to prioritize investment in infrastructure that provides broad public benefit without having to ensure sufficient returns to private investors.

A public infrastructure bank isn't the only type of public banking that would make our economy wealthier and more democratic. The type of bank that most people are familiar with is a depository bank, where individuals and businesses deposit savings and get loans. Most depository banks are private financial institutions, mandated to generate profit for shareholders. But there are other models that are member-owned and democratically governed, such as credit unions and a few cases of state-owned banks. Without the need for shareholder profits, these banks can offer loans at lower cost. Research shows public banks and credit unions are best at supporting regional economic development.

The only remaining publicly owned depository bank in Canada is Alberta Treasury Branch Financial (ATB). In its 2018 report, "Alberta's Public Bank: How ATB Can Help Shape the New Economy," economists Bob Ascah and Mark Anielski draw lessons from the bank's eighty-year history.[11] Ascah (who worked at ATB for over a decade) and Anielski made several proposals to improve ATB's positive social and economic impact and take advantage of its unique features as a public bank, such as offering mortgages at cost to low-income borrowers or targeting strategic supports to renewable energy.

The Canadian Union of Postal Workers (CUPW) has long advocated for extending public banking across Canada, arguing that locating federal public banks in post offices would be an efficient way to extend banking services to underserved and rural communities. The CUPW campaign, Delivering Community Power, links public banking and investment in local communities to address climate change.

Other democratic economic institutions include crown corporations, worker or consumer co-operatives, community-based not-for-profit enterprises and Community Benefit Agreements. Democratic economic institutions have priorities that go beyond profit, which makes them more likely to help generate wealth in our communities and help us transition to a low-carbon economy. As always, the details matter — who the owners are, who benefits from the decisions being made and who is at the decision-making table.

Student Loans and Baby Bonuses

Wealth accumulated in one generation improves things for the next generation. Wealthy parents provide a level of economic security for their children that opens up possibilities in education, unpaid internships, artistic endeavours, or entrepreneurship that would be too risky for most Canadians. Wealthy parents have extensive networks that open doors closed to others and knowledge about how to navigate behind those doors. More directly, well-off baby boomers have been helping their children get into an overheated housing market that shuts out most young Canadians.

At the other end of the spectrum, those blocked from accumulating resources in one generation transmit their experience to the next generation in terms of education, income and wealth inequality. The likelihood that children can do better or worse than their parents is called "intergenerational mobility." Research by Statistics Canada shows that intergenerational mobility in Canada has been declining since the 1970s.[12] Miles Corak, a professor at City University of New York (CUNY) and expert on inequality in Canada, has dubbed this the "Great Gatsby Curve."[13]

Canada has little information about wealth inequality between racialized groups here, because we are only starting to expand data collection on this important aspect of inequality. A Canadian Centre for Policy Alternatives (CCPA) report, *Canada's Colour-Coded Income Inequality,* used 2016 census data to provide a snapshot, looking at investment income returns from capital gains by racialized groups.[14] The CCPA researchers found that a higher proportion of white Canadians had investment income or capital gains than racialized Canadians and they also had a higher average return. The average amount of capital gains was 29 per cent higher for white Canadians and the average investment income was 47 per cent higher.[15] While this is just a snapshot that shows us the returns to some types of investments, it makes it clear that wealth inequality has racial dimensions in Canada, just as it does in the US and other countries.

The CCPA report finds that wealth inequality in previous generations has played a role in creating current income inequality among racialized groups. They argue that precarity, low incomes and poor health outcomes are linked to both race and class and that we must consider both when trying to formulate solutions to economic inequality in Canada.

Experts in the US have suggested that one way to break the cycle of wealth inequality is to transfer wealth to the next generation through the forgiveness of student loan debt, or targeted baby bonds. American economist Darrick Hamilton has proposed that an endowment be given to each child, on a sliding scale based on their parents' wealth and that the child receive the endowment when they reach adulthood. Public health experts in Canada have proposed funding such a program here with a wealth tax.[16]

Although from 2015 to 2019 the Liberals took over $4 billion from some students in interest payments, the federal government continues to charge interest on federal student loans. If the federal government permanently removed interest on all federal student loans, a graduate with a debt of $13,500 (the average such loan) would save $3,357 over the lifetime of the loan. In a context where young people do not have access to the same quality of employment as their parents, where the cost of living is higher and where they cannot even really consider buying a property in many Canadian cities, such a measure would certainly help them make ends meet.

Upholding Indigenous Rights

The money recovered by charging more to those who benefit most from the existing system should also be used to address injustices that have gone on far too long. In 2015, Trudeau campaigned on resolving all long-term drinking water advisories on First Nation reserves within five years. By the end of 2020, one hundred advisories had been lifted, but sixty still remained in place.

A report from Canada's auditor general in February 2021[17] identified several constraints hindering the process, including a flawed federal funding formula for operations and maintenance that makes it nearly impossible for communities to retain trained operators for their water systems. The report concludes, "Overall, Indigenous Services Canada did not provide the support necessary to ensure that First Nations communities have ongoing access to safe drinking water."[18] Upgrading these systems has cost several billion dollars, and now that work has begun in earnest we must also ensure that the federal government covers the ongoing cost of maintaining clean water systems. Ongoing maintenance costs a fraction of the wealth we would generate from the tax proposals outlined here.

Consider how hard it must be for those communities to follow public health advice during the pandemic without drinkable water. Among the sixty communities that still don't have access to drinking water, fourteen of them have been without clean water for more than a decade. In a country as rich as Canada, it is inconceivable that not all Indigenous communities have access to drinking water. If access to drinking water was a problem in Montreal, Toronto, Halifax, or Saskatoon, it would already have been fixed. Asking the super-rich to pay a little bit to ensure all Indigenous people have access to drinking water would change almost nothing for the wealthiest, but it would dramatically change the lives of thousands of Indigenous Canadians.

In 2016, the Canadian Human Rights Tribunal found that Canada discriminated against First Nations children and that First Nations children are often denied services or face long waits for services that other children receive. The ruling covers health care, education, child care, recreation and language services. The federal government disputed the ruling, but the tribunal confirmed it in 2019 and assigned compensation of $40,000 per child affected, as well as $40,000 for parents or other primary caregivers.

The Parliamentary Budget Officer estimated how much it would cost the federal government to comply with this ruling in early 2021, arriving at a range of $4 to $15 billion, depending on the final details of eligibility.[19] Essentially, our federal government has refused to compensate Indigenous children for discriminating against them. The money at issue would only cover basic needs and represents only a small percentage of what we spend on tax cuts for big business.

The Yellowhead Institute, a First Nation–led research centre based in the Faculty of Arts at Ryerson University in Toronto, has written a Red Paper[20] on the Land Back movement, including the ways that Indigenous people have been dispossessed and what communities are doing to assert their rights and jurisdiction.

Approximately 90 per cent of Canada's landmass is considered Crown land — lands claimed by federal or provincial governments (territories come under federal jurisdiction). A significant portion of Canada's wealth comes from resource extraction, and most of that happens on Crown lands — through mining, forestry and hydroelectric dams. First Nations communities across Canada have claimed rights to own, manage and benefit from the wealth generated by Crown lands. Reconciliation will not be possible without addressing land reclamation for Indigenous communities in Canada.

Indigenous people living in communities with long waiting lists for housing make do in overcrowded, dilapidated homes. The term "mould crisis" has been used to describe the depth of the housing health issue. Despite this, the Liberals announced a national housing strategy in 2019 that left behind Indigenous communities.

The list of injustices against Indigenous people is infinitely long. At this point, there should be no more questions about whether we have the finances to make these investments; our governments must simply honour their obligations. For a country as wealthy as Canada, the status quo is unjustifiable. How can we agree, consciously, to offer tax cuts to the top one per cent when we are not able to offer the most essential services to our entire population, especially to Indigenous communities?

What Happens If We Do Nothing?

If we can't stop and ultimately reverse growing wealth and income inequality, we will see more of what we have experienced over the past four decades: more of the same exploitative behaviour from corporations and a continued shrinking role for government. We will see economic inequality, already at disturbing levels, continue to grow. Government will continue to cut taxes, deregulate and divest itself of its important role in shaping markets and addressing discrimination. This means continued wage stagnation, more expensive services and growing social unrest.

We can guess that the near future will look much like the recent past. Wages and incomes for middle- and working-class people have stagnated, while the price of many essential goods like fresh food and shelter have increased faster than inflation. This combination has led to an affordability crisis, with too many Canadians struggling to make ends meet. This dynamic will likely continue.

Two developments in particular have led many Canadians to find life harder in a country that is getting wealthier:

- Unbalanced power in the workplace that allows employers to increase their profits by suppressing wages and imposing poor working conditions.
- Reductions and cutbacks in universal public services that make life easier and more affordable.

Sketchy-but-legal labour practices, such as employers' use of migrant workers on temporary work visas, outsourcing of work to low-wage subcontractors and expanding the use of temp agency workers and contract/gig workers has created a precariat of low-paid, vulnerable, insecure workers. All these measures have shifted wealth from the working class to the owners of capital, and in each case, government has been complicit in failing to protect workers from profit-maximizing and unprincipled employers.

The decline in worker power is often explained as the result of automation and the "new" gig economy — as if these changes are inevitable for workers and we must resign ourselves to their effects. But there is nothing new about how corporations and employers treat workers in the gig economy. There have always been greedy employers who try to shift risk onto workers, impose long hours and unpaid overtime, avoid paying for benefits and fight unionization, all to put more profit into their own pockets. It's the responsibility of democratic institutions, like co-ops, unions and legislatures to ensure that those with money and power cannot so easily exploit workers to become wealthier.

There has been renewed interest in union drives and worker action campaigns in Canada, but after every win, industry lobbyists organize to push back. As of early 2021, no province in Canada (except for a narrow provision in Quebec) had moved to require employer-paid sick days — even though research had shown that this would play a critical role in stopping the spread of COVID-19.[21] Without strong labour standards coupled with active enforcement of those standards, precarious workers remain at the mercy of bad bosses. Economists sometimes call policies to increase workers' rights "predistribution" policies, because they reduce inequality by levelling the playing field within the market.

Public services form part of what is often called the "social wage" — and we have seen erosion in these exactly as families in Canada needed them more. Cutbacks in social housing, social assistance, education and health care along with dramatically rising costs for postsecondary education arrived in tandem with all the tax cuts and loopholes for the wealthy and corporations that we have described in previous chapters. Recent graduates entered unfriendly job markets with escalating debt and diminishing prospects.

Universal public services play an important role in reducing the cost of living and economic inequality, because they disproportionately benefit people who need them. In other words, public services, paid for through fair and progressive taxation, do an excellent job of distributing wealth. The opposite is also true: the absence of public services or inadequate services damage lower-income people most, as they have no choice but to rely on them. Targeting subsidies and public services for certain groups rather than making them universally available often creates stigma and huge gaps that too many people fall through.

The Risk to Our Democracy

As we have noted previously, increasing wealth for the few gives them more and more power, whether it be power as wealthy individuals or as big corporations — either way, their market power ultimately gives them political power. Given the extreme level of wealth inequality we have reached, some individuals or corporations actually have more power than states or jurisdictions.

The more we allow the wealthy to increase their power, the more leverage and influence they will have on political parties like the Conservatives and Liberals. This ultimately leads to tactics aimed at slowing down any measures that could affect their wealth and their profits. The wealthier they are, the more resources they have to influence policy-makers' decisions.

We mentioned in Chapter 9 how in early 2021 Google and Facebook publicly threatened to withdraw their services in Australia if the government went ahead with measures to reduce their profits in that country. Canada is not exempt from this type of blackmail. Indeed, we have already seen big pharmaceutical companies actively stalling and trying to block measures that would reduce the excessive costs of prescription drugs in Canada.

Lower prices are an essential government initiative that could help the majority of Canadians. That's not how big pharma sees it. From 2015, when the federal government began work to change how the ceiling price for patented drugs is set, they threatened to withdraw all research investment in Canada. They also threatened to take the government to court. These threats led the Trudeau government to delay changes, twice, that could make a significant and immediate difference in people's lives.

A second example of big corporations successfully opposing government measures that would benefit Canadians came in the highly regulated telecommunications sector. The "big six" — Telus, Rogers, Shaw, Quebecor's Videotron, Cogeco and Eastlink — threatened to cut back on their "investments" in Canada's telecommunications infrastructure if the government allowed changes that would enable greater competition, resulting in lower service fees.

These are not isolated cases. Many times foreign corporations use the powers defined in trade deals to sue the Canadian government for measures that reduce their profits. The Investor State Dispute Settlement (ISDS) mechanism, found in many Canadian free trade agreements, allows foreign corporate investors to sue governments for decisions that could impact their profits — even if those decisions were designed for the common good, such as environmental regulations, labour regulations, or human rights protection.

If we want to make our system work for the common good rather than for the interests of the richest, we must diminish the growing power that the super-rich and the big corporations have over our democratic institutions. Our democracy is at stake.

Rising Intolerance

Undeniably, Canada's social climate has become more polarized as inequality has increased. More and more people have become radicalized and hate crimes have gone up — criminal incidents motivated by hate and reported to police across Canada rose by more than 60 per cent between 2014 and 2017.

Tolerance, respect, open-mindedness and empathy have become less visible in social interactions. Several factors contribute to this new reality, but growing economic inequalities, lack of trust in our institutions and in our political decision-makers and the feeling that the system is rigged in favour of the few have all undeniably aggravated the situation. Canadians have seen examples of the consequences that such a deteriorated social climate can have in the US, the UK, France and elsewhere in the world.

Canada is not immune to this trend. Some Canadians feel abandoned by their government and sense that nobody is working for them. This attitude is often tied to an individual's quality of life and living conditions, but certainly many Canadians carry strong feelings of abandonment, discouragement and frustration. While many must work two or three jobs to make ends meet, they see Justin Trudeau's Liberal government and previous governments making decisions that consistently benefit the wealthy and big business. They see a wealthy country where a few people grow ever wealthier, while they face a tough struggle economically. When the federal government moves mountains for its corporate friends, everyday Canadians feel left behind.

Several studies have demonstrated the link between economic inequality and social polarization. Feelings of injustice and abandonment make people more vulnerable to populism, misinformation and division. Many politicians, including some in Canada, have tried to channel and fuel that anger with false threats. Sometimes their game is obvious, but at other times it can be subtle. These opportunists will demonize immigrants, other ethnic groups, other nations, women, people in poverty, science and the "traditional media" to create diversion, division and to gain positions of power, where they can implement their policies and slash democratic institutions to stay in power. Such tactics have proven to increase racism, discrimination and hatred.

For example, some politicians attacked Islam, which led to a rise of Islamophobia. Others attacked people of Chinese origin at the beginning of the pandemic, which resulted in targeted assaults on Chinese Canadians.

Elected officials brought to power through tactics of polarization have regularly sought to undermine all legitimate functions of government. When fear of the other is maintained and the system rigged in favour of the most privileged, it becomes more difficult to make progress against the scourges of racism, sexism, and discrimination in all its forms. Such leaders employ diversionary tactics to avoid improving the system. These politicians dismiss the realities that people of colour or Indigenous people face. They will challenge concepts like systemic racism or cultural genocide to delay corrective actions and maintain the status quo. The result is a destructive "culture war," sometimes exacerbated by the other side. Taking real action on the roots of inequality is the only path toward social justice and social peace.

Ultimately, we must remember that the disparate elements of our society are not separated by watertight partitions — they remain intertwined, and they influence one another. Growing economic inequalities threaten our society as a whole — everything is at stake if we don't act.

While societal polarization and radicalization offer no silver lining, creating a fairer society — where wealth is better distributed and people are able to reach their potential through quality public services and an accessible and affordable education system — would certainly greatly improve our social climate. To put it simply, reducing inequalities benefits everyone.

CHAPTER 12

WILL WE SHARE THE WEALTH?

Unrigging the system will not be easy — there will be well-placed and well-funded people and corporations that stand to lose from many of the proposals we have put forward in this book. We have some idea what their playbook will look like, since we have seen it in action.

There are two main paths to opposing political change: prevent it from happening altogether, or propose an alternative that looks like change but isn't really. At the dawn of a discussion on post-COVID-19 economic recovery and at a time when the debt and deficit are historically high, the pressure will be strong to avoid in-depth reforms although they are needed more than ever.

For example, as the pressure for national and universal pharmacare has increased, so has opposition from those who would lose out. While this plan would make most Canadians better off, universal pharmacare would hurt the profits of the pharmaceutical companies. The insurance companies would lose an entire market. The main players have seen that advocates have made a strong case and some kind of change is unavoidable. So rather than oppose pharmacare outright, these two industries actively lobbied the federal government to shift its focus to a hybrid public-private system like the one in Quebec. Let's examine how that system has been working out for Quebecers:

- As of early 2021, Quebecers were paying among the highest per capita prices on prescription drugs and nearly 10 per cent of them could not afford the drugs they need.
- One-third of Quebec households reported paying more than $500 for prescription drugs in 2015, compared to an average of 19 per cent in the rest of Canada.[1]
- Low-income or part-time workers sometimes paid the same private insurance premium as highly paid workers — whether you made $40,000 or $180,000, the average annual premium was $1,334.[2] In addition to the monthly premium, beneficiaries of a private plan in Quebec often have to pay high copayments for their drugs.

All of those challenges can be explained: forcing the public plan to coexist with several private plans deprives the Quebec government of powerful bargaining leverage against pharmaceutical companies. Studies have shown that implementation of a fully public and universal plan could reduce the price of drugs in Canada by 20 to 40 per cent.

Between November 2015 and February 2020, companies in the pharmaceutical industry met with members of the Trudeau government 875 times — an average of eighteen meetings per month. Sympathetic politicians will find ways to delay making any decision, and in this case the government appointed an Advisory Council to undertake a study.

The final report of the Advisory Council regarding implementation of national pharmacare was released in June

2019. Canadians have been considering the idea of universal drug coverage for more than five decades and over that time there has been a high level of consensus on the issue. Still, when NDP Member of Parliament Peter Julian proposed legislation modelled on the Advisory Council's report in February 2021, Liberal members of parliament voted against it — despite having promised universal pharmacare in the 1997 federal election and multiple times afterward, including the 2019 election campaign.

We should not expect Liberals to take meaningful and effective action on any of the measures we have proposed. In early 2021, the Liberals were already laying the groundwork for delay and deferral. Finance Minister Chrystia Freeland's 2021 federal budget only implemented token measures and more consultation on tax fairness. It seemed clear that despite overwhelming public support, the federal Liberals had no intention of making the ultra-rich pay their fair share for the recovery.

Aside from promised investments in child care, the 2021 federal budget reflected the kind of zombie economic thinking that created the economic inequality we describe in Chapter 2 of this book, leaning heavily on tax incentives and the goodwill of private investors to solve public problems. The failure to propose significant measures to share the wealth of Canada's one per cent — and in particularly the very richest Canadian billionaires — was widely noted. The omission was especially glaring since there was widespread support for this approach among the Canadian public and global recognition of the urgent need to address growing inequality. Prime Minister Justin Trudeau and Finance Minister Chrystia Freeland had often acknowledged the issue. There was even a Liberal backbencher, Nathaniel Erskine-Smith, who proposed a one-time tax on the wealthy to help pay for COVID-19 related costs. Instead of meaningful action, the Liberals' 2021 budget proposed higher taxes on expensive boats and cars — an almost meaningless measure that would have virtually no impact on government revenues, or on the super-rich.

If the past is any guide to the future, the message from Liberals and Conservatives in future budgets would be that we need to cut services for people and that we need the middle class and the working class to tighten their belts. Politicians and think tanks can be expected to propose solutions to the government deficit like raising the GST — which everyone has to pay. They may even propose more tax cuts for the richest people or for big business. They will tell us that we need to wait, we need to hold on, they are working on it. Meanwhile they will continue to enable the rigged system — as they have been doing for the last forty years.

The power of corporate lobbyists and their relationships with the Liberals is well documented and does not work in favour of Canadians. It works in favour of private interests, benefits for the few and endless profits for their corporate clients. This has been the case for decades and seems to be deeply rooted in the Liberal way of doing things. The Conservative approach, demonstrated by the Harper government, is to apply strategies that will prevent change altogether.

To change this situation, we really need to speak loud and clear. Insiders and corporate lobbyists are well organized, and often the network of actors fighting against change can be large and interconnected. The Corporate Mapping Project,[3] a major study by Canadian scholars investigating the connections between individuals and companies in the corporate sector and government, has documented how the fossil fuel sector in Canada works and which important players are actively working to slow the transition to green energy.

The project divides the different actors into three categories — three types of actors that we will also have to deal with to achieve a better distribution of wealth in Canada. Here's the breakdown:

1. Emitters — The companies that do the unwanted behaviour, described by the project as "corporations that are directly involved extracting, processing and transporting oil, gas and coal." Enbridge and Husky Energy are good example of emitters.
2. Enablers — The project describes these as "organizations that enable fossil fuel production, such as banks and industry-friendly regulators." The enablers fight change by doubling down on the current system by investing in the unwanted behaviour. Bank of Montreal and Bank of Nova Scotia are two of many examples offered.
3. Legitimators — These are "organizations that persuade the public or political elites that 'business as usual' must continue or that a timely shift away from dependence on fossil fuels is unfeasible or unnecessary." For this category, two think tanks, the CD Howe Institute and the Fraser Institute, offer good examples.

The conclusion elicited by the project's findings? When the interests of the richest are based on an economic sector, the connections are very broad and many actors are involved to either maintain the status quo or slow down the necessary change. None of the actors involved have a vested interest in the system changing, and they will go to great lengths to prevent that from happening.

We must remember that these three categories of actors also have a big microphone. They can count on a lot of news media columnists and commentators who seek to delegitimize or at least question any attempt at change. The usual defenders of the rich and corporate class will shout loudly from their platforms — i.e., Canada's major daily newspapers and nightly pundit television panels — that change is misguided as well as impossible to implement.

An army of commentators, think tanks and sometimes even journalists will attack our proposals using the various myths we talked about earlier that are well entrenched in our society. This is what awaits us — especially in the context of the COVID-19 recovery. When the economic elite feels threatened, they have the resources and power to silence or discredit the threat. Inequality of voice constitutes yet another feature of our rigged system.

It will take many individual Canadians and many organizations allied together to reverse the enormous inequalities that have emerged in this country over the past several decades. But as we have shown throughout the book, many groups, organizations and economists are fighting for this change. Some have been fighting for a long time — and if we organize and mobilize together, we can do it.

The fight for universal medical insurance in Saskatchewan provides a useful example: In 1959, after universal hospital insurance was in place as a jointly funded federal-provincial plan, the governing Co-operative Commonwealth Federation (CCF) announced its plan to launch universal insurance to cover all doctor's visits as well. This became the main issue in the 1960 provincial election. It was fiercely opposed by Canadian and American medical associations and the insurance industry, as well as most provincial media and Chambers of Commerce. Despite an extensive and well-funded propaganda campaign from opponents, the CCF won the election and the legislation implementing universal medical insurance came into effect on July 1, 1962.

That same day, the majority of Saskatchewan's doctors went on strike. Once again, the opposition to public insurance was supported by all kinds of vested interests across North America that wanted to make sure this incredibly popular idea didn't get a toehold. A coalition of farmers, socialists, trade unionists and rank-and-file activists created community clinics in support of doctors who defied the strike. Popular opinion quickly turned against the striking doctors, and they called off the strike three weeks later.[4]

Within ten years of the Saskatchewan doctors' strike, all provinces in Canada had universal medical insurance, bolstered by the idea's popularity and federal funding. More than fifty years later, most Canadians and most Canadian doctors are incredibly proud of our universal medicare. It has made us healthier, our society more equitable and all of us better off than we would be without it.

The fight for ending wealth hoarding has many parallels with the fight for universal medicare. We expect there will be intense opposition from those who benefit from the unfairness in the current system. They will tell us how dangerous change will be and try to convince us that the current rules benefit us too — or that they will some day, when we strike it rich. But if we stick together and remain clear on what we're fighting for, we can win.

And when we do, our whole society will be better off — we'll be healthier and happier, and our economy will be more democratic and fairer. Sharing the wealth isn't an end in and of itself — it's a prerequisite for a prosperous society.

AFTERWORD

WHAT YOU CAN DO TO MAKE IT HAPPEN

It was important for us to write this book because we have seen the impacts of economic inequality in society throughout our lives, and we know that more and more Canadians are now seeing it too. The COVID-19 pandemic exposed long-simmering fault lines of social and economic inequality and inadequate public capacity to address it. Well into the third wave politicians said that they were doing everything they could while disproportionately racialized low-income workers who didn't have paid sick leave were forced to go to work and put their families at risk. This was the case for workers at an Amazon warehouse in Brampton, where workers allege they were forced to go to work even if they were sick, and where an outbreak affected over 600 workers. Meanwhile Amazon was making record profits. Growing numbers of Canadians have seen examples like this and support the types of changes we're proposing.

As parents, we worry for our children. We do not accept that it is inevitable for society to become more unequal, and we refuse to leave this rigged system unchanged for our children. We want to be able to look them in the eye and tell them that we did everything we possibly could to build a fairer society and to not settle for less, to avoid becoming numb and hopeless.

If this resonates within you, if you feel powerless but want to help, if you feel frustrated but want to channel it, then you should keep in mind that we can have strength and power by numbers. There are many ways you can help change the system. The technical changes that we proposed in Part Two will not happen without grassroots agitating and organizing, building the power of the many. We have laid out our proposals to show that change is practical and possible. The only barrier is power.

As we've said a few times already, the richest and most powerful have a lot of power and a lot of means, but what the rest of us have that they don't is strength in numbers. If we want action we must mobilize, organize and put our ideas forward. Victories do not just happen. They are the result of years of hard work and citizen involvement.

Of course, this engagement process is dynamic and varies from one person to another, from one phase of life to another. Everyone can choose their level of commitment, the actions that speak to them most, and the adjustments that best fit them. But if we want things to change, we need to be involved in making change happen.

A great way to take action is to start talking about these issues to the people around you, which is called relational organizing. The idea is that people are more likely to be convinced – to believe evidence or to change their minds – if someone they know talks to them about an issue.

Based on this principle, you can contribute to building a fairer society by making your family, friends, and acquaintances aware of the facts and solutions to economic and social inequality. It is not enough to presume that they know or that they could read about it if they wanted to. The message doesn't get through, and the people in power rely heavily on this. The rich and powerful have the best prime-time platforms to get their message across, so we have to do things differently. You can talk to those around you about ideas that inspire you, things that frustrate you, or what sort of changes you would like to see happen. You can talk about measures you find interesting, inspiring people you follow on social media, or expert insights that struck you. Or you can help debunk the myths outlined in Part One. You can suggest or offer a book to someone, you can share articles on social media, etc. You know your people and you know what makes sense for you. The goal of this approach is that eventually you will be able to talk to your circle about relational organizing and invite them to spread awareness in turn. One person at a time, this strategy allows us to counterbalance the power of the economic elite with the power of numbers. If thousands of us stand up for change, policymakers will be unable to ignore us.

You can also get involved in politics, helping to elect MPs who will fight against inequality. You probably won't be surprised when we tell you that we believe part of the solution lies in the election of politicians who reflect these values and priorities. We've personally chosen the NDP because New Democrats have been powerful advocates for social progress for decades. It is the cornerstone of our movement and its priorities. We may not have the same means to get our message across as the two major parties, but we certainly have the expertise to design and deliver efficient and well-structured policies to improve people's lives. We strongly feel that with more NDP MPs in Parliament, people like us are better represented.

The NDP has earned their nickname as the conscience of the Parliament. Although we have both been involved in politics for many years, we feel this is a rare moment where the right fight can make a significant difference in people's lives. Rising to the occasion is a great privilege and responsibility. Every time the NDP achieves a gain for the people, it proves that ordinary people are better served when they have NDP MPs on their side. Unfortunately, fewer NDP MPs in Parliament means fewer forces to counterbalance those who represent the interests of the wealthiest. Remember that after the 2000 election, the NDP dropped to 13 out of 301 seats, which allowed Jean Chrétien's and Paul Martin's government to cut taxes for the rich almost unchecked.

Regardless of political affiliation, we believe that democratic systems are stronger when voters are engaged in them, so we recommend volunteering for a local candidate who reflects your values. No matter your strength, there is a place and task for everybody. Tasks can take the form of telephone calls, candidate support during elections, social media presence, fundraising and membership drives, photography, events management, writing, translation, graphic design, printing, installation of electoral signs, and many more options. Even a small amount of time can make a difference. Involvement can also take the form of running for office. There are certainly many challenges for candidates, but running for election can be a life-changing experience.

We also recommend supporting community organizations that work to fight inequality every day. Campaigns for sick days, higher minimum wages, poverty eradication, affordable housing, and tenants' rights are only a few of the options you can probably find in your community. Unions are also a great example of everyday people challenging inequalities by fighting for better working conditions and pushing governments to invest in public services and social programs. Getting involved in a union is also an effective way to help tackle inequalities and improve people's lives.

Both community engagement and political commitment are powerful channels to combat powerlessness and frustration within a system that is not working as it should. The key here, as rapper Killer Mike said after the protests surrounding the death of George Floyd, is to "plot, plan, strategize, organize and mobilize."[1] Change will inevitably require involvement and mobilization.

We are at a critical juncture and we need your help to build a fairer country. There is hope, but it requires all of us to work together. We hope that with this book we have convinced you that this change is possible. The battle in front of us will not be easy, but we have no choice but to continue to fight. Society and the economy will not hold together if our country's growing wealth continues to benefit the wealthiest while the rest of us, the 99 per cent, are abandoned or asked to wait. The same goes for our democracy. If the majority of our voices continue to be ignored, our democracy will eventually collapse. If we want better, we must fight for it — the rich and powerful and those who listen to them will not give it to us on a golden platter. Let's get to work.

— J.G. and A.M.

ACKNOWLEDGEMENTS

First and foremost, we would like to thank our partners, Sara Nadon and Isaac Tamblyn. They were instrumental in reviewing drafts, talking through ideas and supporting us through the process of writing and editing. Crystal Regier and Laura Davies provided thoughtful reflections on the ideas we discuss in the book and much appreciated emotional support.

While we were writing the first draft, Angella spent several weeks with her brother, Ryan, who was in palliative care at Saint Paul's Hospital in Saskatoon, Saskatchewan. Angella would like to thank the staff at Saint Paul's for their excellent care and for several good conversations on the political economy of taxing the rich.

The ideas we present in this book have been developed in discussion with colleagues over several years. We would especially like to thank Andrew Jackson, Armine Yalnizyan, Christine Saulnier, Jonathan Sas, Jordan Leichnitz, Karin Jordan, Lars Osberg, Peggy Nash, Rob Gillezeau and Toby Sanger and everyone who participates in the Progressive Economics Forum. Any errors or flaws in the work or our logic are of course ours alone.

We would also like to thank Jim Lorimer for his interest in this project and his enthusiastic support at every step. Thanks to Cecilia Stuart for being our guide and the rest of the staff at Lorimer who helped bring everything together for the book.

Finally, we would like to respectfully acknowledge that we researched and wrote this book on Treaty 6 territory and the homeland of the Métis and on the unceded territory of the Algonquin Anishinaabeg.

REFERENCES

All hyperlinks were checked for functionality on April 23, 2021.

Chapter 1

1. Jonathan D. Ostry, Prakash Loungani, and Andrew Berg. *Confronting Inequality*. Columbia University Press, 2019.
2. Rupert Neate, "Billionaires' wealth rises to $10.2 trillion amid Covid crisis," *The Guardian*, October 7, 2020. https://www.theguardian.com/business/2020/oct/07/covid-19-crisis-boosts-the-fortunes-of-worlds-billionaires
3. Oxfam, *Public Good or Private Wealth?*, January 2019. https://42kgab3z3i7s3rm1xf48rq44-wpengine.netdna-ssl.com/wp-content/uploads/2019/01/Public-Good-or-Private-Wealth-FINAL-en.pdf.
4. Ibid.
5. Samuel Stebbins and Grant Suneson, "Jeff Bezos, Elon Musk among US billionaires getting richer during coronavirus pandemic," *USA Today*, December 1, 2020. https://www.usatoday.com/story/money/2020/12/01/american-billionaires-that-got-richer-during-covid/43205617.
6. Ibid.
7. Rupert Neate, "Billionaires' wealth rises to $10.2 trillion amid Covid crisis," *The Guardian*, October 7, 2020. https://www.theguardian.com/business/2020/oct/07/covid-19-crisis-boosts-the-fortunes-of-worlds-billionaires.
8. World Bank. *Poverty and Share Prosperity 2020: Reversals of Fortune*. World Bank, 2020. https://openknowledge.worldbank.org/bitstream/handle/10986/34496/211602ov.pdf.
9. Office of the Parliamentary Budget Officer. "*Estimating the Top Tail of the Family Wealth Distribution in Canada*," June 17, 2020. https://www.pbo-dpb.gc.ca/web/default/files/Documents/Reports/RP-2021-007-S/RP-2021-007-S_en.pdf.
10. David Macdonald. *Born to Win: Wealth concentration in Canada since 1999*. CCPA, 2018. http://www.policyalternatives.ca/sites/default/files/uploads/publications/National%20Office/2018/07/Born%20to%20Win.pdf.
11. Ibid.
12. Alex Hemingway. "One year later: Canadian billionaire wealth up by $78 billion." *Policy Note*, April 2021. https://www.policynote.ca/the-rich-and-the-rest-of-us.
13. Derrick O'Keefe, "COVID sucks, unless you're a billionaire. Canada's richest have raked in $37 billion since March," *Ricochet*, September 17, 2020. https://ricochet.media/en/3286/covid-sucks-unless-youre-a-billionaire-canadas-richest-rake-in-37-billion-since-march.
14. Forbes Magazine publishes an annual list of the world's billionaires wealth every March, and provides real-time updates at the close of markets each day online at forbes.com/real-time-billionaires. The amounts we cite here were calculated based

on the difference between Forbes' estimate of each billionaire's wealth in March and on December 31st, 2020, and have been converted to Canadian dollars by the authors.

15. David Macdonald. *Born to Win: Wealth concentration in Canada since 1999.* CCPA, 2018. http://www.policyalternatives.ca/sites/default/files/uploads/publications/National%20Office/2018/07/Born%20to%20Win.pdf.
16. David Macdonald. *Climbing Up and Kicking Down: Executive Pay in Canada.* CCPA, 2018. https://www.policyalternatives.ca/sites/default/files/uploads/publications/National%20Office/2018/01/Climbing%20Up%20and%20Kicking%20Down.pdf.
17. For more information, see: https://www.atco.com/en-ca/about-us/governance/board-directors.html.
18. For more information, see: https://www.sprucemeadows.com/history.
19. David Macdonald. *The Golden Cushion: CEO compensation in Canada.* CCPA, 2021. https://www.policyalternatives.ca/sites/default/files/uploads/publications/National%20Office/2021/01/Golden%20cushion.pdf.
20. Statistics Canada. Table 11-10-0008-01: Tax filers and dependants with income by total income, sex and age.
21. Statistics Canada. Table 11-10-0055-01: High income tax filers in Canada.
22. The Statistics Canada table on High income tax filers in Canada tells us the average market income, and the average market income including capital gains for each income group. Subtracting one from the other gives us the average market income from capital gains.
23. Valerie Tarasuk and Andy Mitchell. *Household food insecurity in Canada, 2017-18.* PROOF, 2020. https://proof.utoronto.ca/resources/proof-annual-reports/household-food-insecurity-in-canada-2017-2018.
24. Angus Reid. "What does poverty look like in Canada? Survey finds one-in-four experience notable economic hardship", July 17, 2018.
25. It is important to note that the actual number is potentially much higher, given that many people who are unhoused live with friends or relatives, and do not come into contact with emergency shelters. Data from a Ipsos Reid poll in March 2013 suggests that as many as 1.3 million Canadians have experienced homelessness or extremely insecure housing at some point during the past five years. For more information, see: https://www.homelesshub.ca/about-homelessness/homelessness-101/how-many-people-are-homeless-canada.
26. There were 4.4 million people in low income according to the Low Income Measure after tax in 2018. See: Statistics Canada. Table 11-10-0135-01: Low income statistics by age, sex and economic family type
27. Statistics Canada. "Labour Force Survey, January 2021," February 5, 2021. https://www.150.statcan.gc.ca/n1/daily-quotidien/210205/dq210205a-eng.htm.
28. Alex Hemingway and Michal Rozworski, "Canadian billionaires' wealth skyrocketing amid the pandemic," Policy Note, September 16, 2020. https://www.policynote.ca/billionaires-wealth.
29. La Presse canadienne, "La COVID-19 creuse l'écart entre les riches et les pauvres

au Canada," *Radio-Canada*, February 20, 2021. https://ici.radio-canada.ca/nouvelle/1772247/chomage-economie-canada-perte-emploi-faible-revenu?fbclid=IwAR3qBtrq45BrA7QuSvVl7BTS20aoW_6uhjHbXFrtMNX_k3GDtxjme4g18jI.

30. Jonathan Montpetit, Simon Nakonechny, and Marie-Hélène Hétu, "Why millions of dollars in pandemic aid is going to corporations making healthy profits," *CBC News*, December 10, 2020. https://www.cbc.ca/news/canada/montreal/cews-wage-subsidy-jobs-covid-1.5834790.
31. Kenyon Wallace, Ed Tubb, Marco Chown Oved, "Big for-profit long-term-care companies paid out more than $170 million to investors through Ontario's deadly first wave," *Toronto Star*, December 26, 2020. https://www.thestar.com/news/gta/2020/12/26/big-for-profit-long-term-care-companies-paid-out-more-than-170-million-to-investors-through-ontarios-deadly-first-wave.html.
32. Credit Suisse Research Institute. *Global Wealth Databook 2019*. Credit Suisse, October 2019. Table 7.5.
33. Andrew Jackson. *The Return of the Gilded Age: Consequences, Causes and Solutions*. The Harry Kitchen Lecture in Public Policy, Trent University, April 8, 2015. https://d3n8a8pro7vhmx.cloudfront.net/broadbent/pages/7725/attachments/original/1592497036/The_Return_of_the_Gilded_Age.pdf?1592497036.
34. Hoskins et al. *Final Report of the Advisory Council on the Implementation of National Pharmacare*. June 2019.
35. Ibid.
36. Ruth Lopert, Elizabeth Docteur, and Steve Morgan. *Body Count: The human cost of financial barriers to prescription medications*. Canadian Federation of Nurses Unions, May 2018. https://nursesunions.ca/research/body-count.
37. HealthCareCan. *Towards a national pharmacare program: Consideration for Canadian Healthcare Organizations*. February 2019.
38. Statistics Canada. "Dental Care, 2018," *Health Fact Sheets*. September 2019. https://www150.statcan.gc.ca/n1/pub/82-625-x/2019001/article/00010-eng.htm.
39. Rupert Neate, "World's witnessing a new Gilded Age as billionaires' wealth swells to $6tn," *The Guardian*, October 26, 2017. https://www.theguardian.com/business/2017/oct/26/worlds-witnessing-a-new-gilded-age-as-billionaires-wealth-swells-to-6tn.
40. Ibid.
41. See Chapter 2 - *Toward a More Dismal Economy* in Joseph E. Stiglitz. *People, Power, and Profits*. WW Norton, 2019.
42. Eric D. Gould and Alexander Hijzen. *Growing Apart, Losing Trust? The Impact of Inequality on Social Capital*, IMF Working Paper, 2016. https://www.imf.org/external/pubs/ft/wp/2016/wp16176.pdf.
43. P. Fajnzylber, D. Lederman and N. Loayza. "Inequality and Violent Crime." *Journal of Law and Economics*, 2002 45(1):1–40; Wilkinson and Pickett. The Spirit Level. Penguin, 2009.
44. Wilkinson and Pickett. *The Inner Level*. Penguin, 2018.
45. Council on Foreign Relations. *Inequality and the rise of Authoritarianism*. Transcript of panel featuring Jack A. Goldstone, Kathleen R. McNamara and Shadi

Hamid, February 23, 2017. https://www.cfr.org/event/inequality-and-rise-authoritarianism.
46. Oxfam, *Public Good or Private Wealth?*, January 2019.
47. Andrew Jackson. *Multi-Millionaires and Fair Taxes: The Case for a Wealth Tax in Canada*. Broadbent Institute, June 2020. https://d3n8a8pro7vhmx.cloudfront.net/broadbent/pages/7711/attachments/original/1592491105/The_Case_for_a_Wealth_Tax_in_Canada_-_Report.pdf.
48. See Chapter 3 – *Exploitation and Market Power* in Joseph E. Stiglitz. People, Power, and Profits. WW Norton, 2019.
49. See Chapter 8 in Lars Osberg, *The Age of Increasing Inequality: The Astonishing Rise of Canada's 1%*. Lorimer, 2018
50. The Liberal government has again promised to act with a watered-down solution in its fall 2020 economic update. At the time of writing this book, no concrete action to implement these changes has been taken and it was impossible to tell whether this time action would be taken, or if for a second time the idea would be blocked by the lobbyists and the beneficiaries.
51. Oxfam, *Public Good or Private Wealth?*, January 2019.
52. Tim Gore, Mira Alestig, and Anna Ratcliff. *Confronting Carbon Inequality*. Oxfam, 2020. https://oxfamilibrary.openrepository.com/bitstream/handle/10546/621052/mb-confronting-carbon-inequality-210920-en.pdf.
53. United Nations Environment Programme. *Emissions Gap Report 2020*. https://wedocs.unep.org/xmlui/bitstream/handle/20.500.11822/34426/EGR20.pdf.
54. Matt McGrath. "Climate change: Global 'elite' will need to slash high-carbon lifestyles," *BBC News*, December 9, 2020. https://www.bbc.com/news/science-environment-55229725.

Chapter 2

1. Thomas Piketty. *The Economics of Inequality*. Translated by Arthur Goldhammer. Belknap Press, 2015. pg.1-5
2. Mara Liasson, "Conservative Advocate." *NPR Morning Edition*. May 25, 2001. https://www.npr.org/templates/story/story.php?storyId=1123439.
3. See Chapter 3 – *Exploitation and Market Power* in Joseph E. Stiglitz. *People, Power and Profits*. WW Norton, 2019.
4. Ibid.
5. Ibid.
6. Mariana Mazzucato. *The Entrepreneurial State: Debunking Public vs. Private Sector Myths*. Anthem Press, 2013.
7. See Chapter 6 – *The Crisis in Economics* in Paul Krugman. *Arguing with Zombies.* WW Norton, 2019.
8. See Chapter 8 in Lars Osberg. *The Age of Increasing Inequality: The Astonishing Rise of Canada's 1%*. Lorimer, 2018.
9. Facundo Alvaredo, Lucas Chancel, Thomas Piketty, Emmanuel Saez, Gabriel Zucman. *The World Inequality Report 2018*. World Inequality Lab, 2017. https://wir2018.wid.world.

10. Armine Yalnizyan. *Inclusive growth and the future of work: 2017 Rosenbluth Lecture.* CCPA BC, 2017.
11. Hugh MacKenzie. *The Great CEO Pay Race.* CCPA, 2008. https://www.policyalternatives.ca/sites/default/files/uploads/publications/National_Office_Pubs/2008/The_Great_CEO_Pay_Race.pdf.
12. David Macdonald. *The Golden Cushion: CEO compensation in Canada.* CCPA, 2021. https://www.policyalternatives.ca/sites/default/files/uploads/publications/National%20Office/2021/01/Golden%20cushion.pdf.
13. See Chapter 3 – *Exploitation and Market Power* in Joseph E. Stiglitz. *People, Power and Profits.* WW Norton, 2019.
14. Andrew Jackson. *The Return of the Gilded Age: Consequences, Causes and Solutions.* The Harry Kitchen Lecture in Public Policy, Trent University, April 8, 2015.
15. Lars Osberg. *The Age of Increasing Inequality: The Astonishing Rise of Canada's 1%.* Lorimer, 2018. pg.143.
16. Kate Raworth. *Doughnut Economics: Seven Ways to Think Like a 21st-Century Economist.* Random House, 2017.
17. See Chapter 10 - *Tax Cuts* in Paul Krugman. *Arguing with Zombies.* WW Norton, 2019.
18. David Hope and Julian Limberg. "The Economic Consequences of Major Tax Cuts for the Rich," London School of Economics International Inequities Institute, December 2020. http://eprints.lse.ac.uk/107919/1/Hope_economic_consequences_of_major_tax_cuts_published.pdf.
19. Craig Stirling. "Fifty Years of Tax Cuts for Rich Didn't Trickle Down, Study Says," *Bloomberg*, December 15, 2020. https://www.bloomberg.com/news/articles/2020-12-16/fifty-years-of-tax-cuts-for-rich-didn-t-trickle-down-study-says.
20. See Chapter 10 - *Tax Cuts* in Paul Krugman. *Arguing with Zombies.* WW Norton, 2019.
21. "The economic contribution of the CCB to Canada's economy is substantial. Over the course of the program's existence, the CCB's contribution to GDP amounts to 2.1% of Canada's total GDP. Every $1 disbursed through the program to Canadian families has translated to a $1.97 contribution to GDP, meaning that the economic activity generated by the CCB is almost twice the size of the CCB payments themselves. This economic stimulus also generates tax revenue which can help offset the cost of the program. For every $1 disbursed to Canadian families through the CCB, over half ($0.55) is recuperated through taxes, $0.30 to the federal government and $0.25 to provincial governments." https://www.cancea.ca/CCB.
22. See Chapter 3 – *Exploitation and Market Power* in Joseph E. Stiglitz. *People, Power and Profits.* WW Norton, 2019.
23. David Macdonald. "Corporate tax cuts enrich shareholders, not competitiveness," *The Monitor*, November 21, 2018. https://monitormag.ca/articles/corporate-tax-cuts-enrich-shareholders-not-competitiveness.
24. Ibid.
25. Ibid.
26. Ibid.

27. Canadian Press. "Oilsands companies boost Q2 net incomes by $2 billion thanks to Alberta tax cuts," *CBC News*, July 25, 2019. https://www.cbc.ca/news/canada/calgary/oilsands-companies-boost-q2-net-incomes-by-2-billion-thanks-to-alberta-tax-cuts-1.5225041.
28. Marco Chown Oved, Toby A.A. Heaps, Michael Yow. "The High Cost of Low Corporate Tax Rates," *Toronto Star*, December 14, 2017. https://projects.thestar.com/canadas-corporations-pay-less-tax-than-you-think.
29. See Introduction in Paul Krugman. *Arguing with Zombies.* WW Norton, 2019.
30. David Macdonald. *Born to Win: Wealth concentration in Canada since 1999.* CCPA, 2018. http://www.policyalternatives.ca/sites/default/files/uploads/publications/National%20Office/2018/07/Born%20to%20Win.pdf.
31. OECD. *The Role and Design of Net Wealth Taxes in the OECD*, OECD Tax Policy Studies, 2018. http://www.oecd.org/ctp/the-role-and-design-of-net-wealth-taxes-in-the-oecd-9789264290303-en.htm.
32. Andrew Jackson. *Multi-Millionaires and Fair Taxes: The Case for a Wealth Tax in Canada.* Broadbent Institute, June 2020. https://d3n8a8pro7vhmx.cloudfront.net/broadbent/pages/7711/attachments/original/1592491105/The_Case_for_a_Wealth_Tax_in_Canada_-_Report.pdf?1592491105.
33. Andrew Jackson and Toby Sanger, "Policy Forum: The Case for an Annual Net Wealth Tax," *Canadian Tax Journal*, 2020. 68:3, 835 – 50. https://www.ctf.ca/CTFWEB/Documents/CTJ%202020/Issue%203/835_2020CTJ3-PF-Jackson-Sanger.pdf.
34. Thomas Piketty. *Capital and Ideology*. The Belknap Press, 2020.
35. Rupert Neate, "Billionaires' wealth rises to $10.2 trillion amid Covid crisis," *The Guardian*, October 7, 2020. https://www.theguardian.com/business/2020/oct/07/covid-19-crisis-boosts-the-fortunes-of-worlds-billionaires.

Chapter 3

1. Andrew Jackson. *The Return of the Gilded Age: Consequences, Causes and Solutions.* The Harry Kitchen Lecture in Public Policy, Trent University, April 8, 2015. https://d3n8a8pro7vhmx.cloudfront.net/broadbent/pages/7725/attachments/original/1592497036/The_Return_of_the_Gilded_Age.pdf?1592497036.
2. Ibid.
3. Ibid.
4. OECD (2021), Unit labour costs (indicator). doi: 10.1787/37d9d925-en.
5. Andrew Jackson. *The Return of the Gilded Age: Consequences, Causes and Solutions.* The Harry Kitchen Lecture in Public Policy, Trent University, April 8, 2015. https://d3n8a8pro7vhmx.cloudfront.net/broadbent/pages/7725/attachments/original/1592497036/The_Return_of_the_Gilded_Age.pdf?1592497036.
6. Michal Rozworski, "Canada's Harsh 'Austerity' Policies Started with Liberals," *The Tyee*, August 25, 2015. https://thetyee.ca/Opinion/2015/08/25/Canadas-Harsh-Austeritz.
7. Ibid.
8. Andrew Jackson, "Beware the Canadian Austerity Model: Europeans should shun

Paul Martin's deficit-cutting ways," *The Monitor*, June 1, 2010. https://www.policyalternatives.ca/publications/monitor/beware-canadian-austerity-model.
9. Brian Murphy, Mike Veall, and Michael Wolfson, "Top-End Progressivity and Federal Tax Preferences in Canada: Estimates from Personal Income Tax Data," *Canadian Tax Journal*, 2015. 63.3, 661-88.
10. Andrew Jackson and Toby Sanger, "Policy Forum: The Case for an Annual Net Wealth Tax," *Canadian Tax Journal*, 2020. 68:3, 835 – 50. https://www.ctf.ca/CTFWEB/Documents/CTJ%202020/Issue%203/835_2020CTJ3-PF-Jackson-Sanger.pdf.
11. Marco Chown Oved, Toby A.A. Heaps, Michael Yow. "The High Cost of Low Corporate Tax Rates," *Toronto Star*, December 14, 2017. https://projects.thestar.com/canadas-corporations-pay-less-tax-than-you-think.
12. Ibid.
13. Toby Sanger. "Time to step up for tax justice," *The Monitor*, November 1, 2019. https://www.policyalternatives.ca/publications/monitor/time-step-tax-justice.
14. Diane Francis. "The U.S. is finally doing something about the global money laundering scourge. Will we?" *Financial Post*, December 10, 2020. https://financialpost.com/diane-francis/diane-francis-the-u-s-is-finally-doing-something-about-the-global-money-laundering-scourge-will-we.
15. Toby Sanger. "Time to step up for tax justice," *The Monitor*, November 1, 2019. https://www.policyalternatives.ca/publications/monitor/time-step-tax-justice.
16. Ibid.
17. Andrew Jackson and Toby Sanger, "Policy Forum: The Case for an Annual Net Wealth Tax," *Canadian Tax Journal*, 2020. 68:3, 835 – 50. https://www.ctf.ca/CTFWEB/Documents/CTJ%202020/Issue%203/835_2020CTJ3-PF-Jackson-Sanger.pdf.
18. Parliamentary Budget Officer, "Preliminary Findings on International Taxation," 2019. https://www.pbo-dpb.gc.ca/web/default/files/Documents/Reports/2019/Preliminary-Findings-International-Taxation/Report%20final.pdf.

Chapter 4

1. Andrew Jackson. *Multi-Millionaires and Fair Taxes: The Case for a Wealth Tax in Canada*. Broadbent Institute, June 2020. https://d3n8a8pro7vhmx.cloudfront.net/broadbent/pages/7711/attachments/original/1592491105/The_Case_for_a_Wealth_Tax_in_Canada_-_Report.pdf?1592491105.
2. Ibid.
3. Andrew Jackson and Toby Sanger, "Policy Forum: The Case for an Annual Net Wealth Tax," *Canadian Tax Journal*, 2020. 68:3, 835 – 50. https://www.ctf.ca/CTFWEB/Documents/CTJ%202020/Issue%203/835_2020CTJ3-PF-Jackson-Sanger.pdf.
4. Joseph Zeballos-Roig, "4 European countries still have a wealth tax. Here's how much success they've each had." Business Insider, November 7, 2019. https://www.businessinsider.com/4-european-countries-wealth-tax-spain-norway-switzerland-belgium-2019-11.

5. *BBC News*. "Covid: Argentina passes tax on wealthy to pay for virus measures," *BBC News*, December 5, 2020. https://www.bbc.com/news/world-latin-america-55199058.
6. Bloomberg. "The wealth tax is going global," Business Insider, January 9, 2021. https://www.businesstimes.com.sg/wealth-investing/the-wealth-tax-is-going-global.
7. Arun Advani, Emma Chamberlain, and Andy Summers. "A wealth tax for the UK," *Wealth Tax Commission*. December 9, 2020. https://www.wealthandpolicy.com/wp/WealthTaxFinalReport.pdf.
8. Parliamentary Budget Officer. "Net Wealth Tax," Office of the Parliamentary Budget Officer, September 10, 2019. https://www.pbo-dpb.gc.ca/web/default/files/Documents/ElectionProposalCosting/Results/32630202_EN.pdf.
9. Alex Hemingway. "Wealth tax would raise far more money than previously thought," Policy Note, March 11, 2021. policynote.ca/tax-the-rich.
10. Elizabeth Warren. *Ultra-millionaire Tax*. https://elizabethwarren.com/plans/ultra-millionaire-tax.
11. Star Editorial Board. "Billionaires get richer while millions struggle. There's a lot wrong with this picture," *Toronto Star*, September 21, 2020. https://www.thestar.com/opinion/editorials/2020/09/21/billionaires-get-richer-while-millions-struggle-theres-a-lot-wrong-with-this-picture.html.
12. Bruce Anderson and David Coletto, "Wealth tax? Canadians like the idea." *Abacus Data*, November 19, 2020. https://abacusdata.ca/wealth-tax-canada-poll.
13. The record of votes on Peter Julian's Opposition Motion - Tax measures to support Canadians - is available online: https://www.ourcommons.ca/members/en/votes/43/2/22.
14. Andrew Jackson and Toby Sanger, "Policy Forum: The Case for an Annual Net Wealth Tax," *Canadian Tax Journal*, 2020. 68:3, 835 – 50 https://www.ctf.ca/CTFWEB/Documents/CTJ%202020/Issue%203/835_2020CTJ3-PF-Jackson-Sanger.pdf.
15. OECD. *The Role and Design of Net Wealth Taxes in the OECD*. 2018. https://www.oecd.org/tax/tax-policy/role-and-design-of-net-wealth-taxes-in-the-OECD-summary.pdf.

Chapter 5

1. Linda McQuaig. *Behind Closed Doors: How the Rich Won Control of Canada's Tax System ... and Ended Up Richer*. Viking Press, 1987.
2. David Macdonald. *The Golden Cushion: CEO compensation in Canada*. CCPA, 2021. https://www.policyalternatives.ca/sites/default/files/uploads/publications/National%20Office/2021/01/Golden%20cushion.pdf.
3. Brian Murphy, Mike Veall, and Michael Wolfson, "Top-End Progressivity and Federal Tax Preferences in Canada: Estimates from Personal Income Tax Data," *Canadian Tax Journal*, 2015. 63.3, 661-88. https://papers.ssrn.com/sol3/papers.cfm?abstract_id=2692788.
4. Finance Canada. *Report on Federal Tax Expenditures, 2020*. https://www.canada.ca/content/dam/fin/publications/taxexp-depfisc/2020/taxexp-depfisc20-eng.pdf.

5. Ibid.
6. Parliamentary Budget Officer. "Raising the Inclusion Rate of Capital Gains for taxation," October 11, 2019. https://www.pbo-dpb.gc.ca/web/default/files/Documents/ElectionProposalCosting/Results/32917623_EN.pdf?timestamp=1610412386128.
7. Dennis Howlett, "Stock Options: The Billion dollar Loophole," *Canadians for Tax Fairness*, March 2014. https://www.taxfairness.ca/en/news/stock-options-billion-dollar-tax-loophole.
8. PressProgress, "Bill Morneau Flip-Flops on His Flip-Flop, Promises to Finally 'Take Action' on CEO Stock Options Tax Loophole," March 19, 2019. https://pressprogress.ca/bill-morneau-flip-flops-on-his-flip-flop-promises-to-finally-take-action-on-ceo-stock-options-tax-loophole.
9. Canadian Centre for Policy Alternatives, "High CEO pay shatters previous records, now 227 times more than average worker pay," January 2, 2020. https://www.policyalternatives.ca/newsroom/news-releases/high-ceo-pay-shatters-previous-records-now-227-times-more-average-worker-pay.
10. PressProgress, "Bill Morneau Flip-Flops on His Flip-Flop, Promises to Finally 'Take Action' on CEO Stock Options Tax Loophole," March 19, 2019. https://pressprogress.ca/bill-morneau-flip-flops-on-his-flip-flop-promises-to-finally-take-action-on-ceo-stock-options-tax-loophole.
11. Finance Canada. *Report on Federal Tax Expenditures, 2020*. https://www.canada.ca/content/dam/fin/publications/taxexp-depfisc/2020/taxexp-depfisc20-eng.pdf.
12. Sean Silcoff, "Liberals drop controversial stock options tax plan," *The Globe and Mail*, March 22, 2016. https://www.theglobeandmail.com/report-on-business/small-business/startups/liberals-drop-controversial-stock-options-tax-plan/article29337792.
13. Parliamentary Budget Officer. "Change in the tax treatment of employee stock options," January 14, 2021. https://pbo-dpb.s3.ca-central1.amazonaws.com/artefacts/aa718780da5b1fb204b35701bba4d81bbd9d11e68895292f28ea617b43776c1d.
14. Parliamentary Budget Officer. "Eliminating the tax deduction for employee stock option," October 11, 2019. https://www.pbo-dpb.gc.ca/web/default/files/Documents/ElectionProposalCosting/Results/33205786_EN.pdf.
15. PressProgress. "Tax Loophole Used For Corporate Entertainment Will Cost Canada $200 Million This Year," February 15, 2018. https://pressprogress.ca/tax-loophole-used-for-corporate-entertainment-will-cost-canada-200-million-this-year.
16. Finance Canada. *Report on Federal Tax Expenditures, 2020*. https://www.canada.ca/content/dam/fin/publications/taxexp-depfisc/2020/taxexp-depfisc20-eng.pdf.

Chapter 6

1. Lars Osberg. *How Much Tax Could Canada's Top 1% Pay*. CCPA, 2015. https://www.policyalternatives.ca/sites/default/files/uploads/publications/National%20Office/2015/10/How_Much_Tax_Could_Canadas_Top_1_Pay.pdf.

2. Armine Yalnizyan. *The Rise of Canada's Top 1%*. CCPA, 2010. https://www.policyalternatives.ca/sites/default/files/uploads/publications/National%20Office/2010/12/Richest%201%20Percent.pdf.
3 Ibid.
4. Emmanuel Saez and Michael Veall, "The Evolution of High Incomes in Northern America: Lessons from Canadian Evidence", *American Economic Review*, 2005, 95(3), pp. 831–849.
5. Statistics Canada. Table 11-10-0058-01 - Federal and provincial effective tax rates of census families
6. Osberg, Lars. *How Much Tax Could Canada's Top 1% Pay*. CCPA, 2015. https://www.policyalternatives.ca/sites/default/files/uploads/publications/National%20 Office/2015/10/How_Much_Tax_Could_Canadas_Top_1_Pay.pdf.
7. Ibid.
8. Gustav Fritzon and Jacob Lundberg, "Taxing High Incomes – A Comparison of 41 Countries," *EPICENTER*, 2019. https://files.taxfoundation.org/20191022160341/Taxing-High-Income-A-Comparison-of-41-Countries-PDF.pdf.
9. Ibid.
10. Parliamentary Budget Officer. "Change in federal tax rate for high income earners from 33% to 35%." October 11, 2019. https://www.pbo-dpb.gc.ca/web/default/files/Documents/ElectionProposalCosting/Results/32630416_EN.pdf.
11. See Chapter 8 – *Restoring Democracy* in Joseph E. Stiglitz. *People, Power and Profits*. WW Norton, 2019.

Chapter 7

1. See Chapter 1 – *What we know* in Alain Deneault. *Legalizing theft*. Les Éditions Écosociétés, 2016.
2. Ibid.
3. Ibid.
4. Ibid.
5. Toby Sanger. "Time to step up for tax justice," *The Monitor*, November 1, 2019. https://www.policyalternatives.ca/publications/monitor/time-step-tax-justice.
6. Zach Dubinsky, "How Canada got into bed with tax havens," *CBC News*, June 18, 2016. https://www.cbc.ca/news/business/canada-offshore-treaties-barbados-tax-avoidance-1.3641278.
7. Toby Sanger. "Time to step up for tax justice," *The Monitor*, November 1, 2019. https://www.policyalternatives.ca/publications/monitor/time-step-tax-justice.
8. Zach Dubinsky, "How Canada got into bed with tax havens," *CBC News*, June 18, 2016. https://www.cbc.ca/news/business/canada-offshore-treaties-barbados-tax-avoidance-1.3641278.
9. Ibid.
10. Ibid.
11. Marco Chown Oved, Toby A.A. Heaps, Michael Yow. "The High Cost of Low Corporate Tax Rates," *Toronto Star*, December 14, 2017. https://projects.thestar.com/canadas-corporations-pay-less-tax-than-you-think.

12. Canadians for Tax Fairness, "Canadian corporate assets in tax havens reach new high of $381 Billion," July 22. 2020. https://www.taxfairness.ca/en/press_release/2020-07/media-release-canadian-corporate-assets-tax-havens-reach-new-high-381-billion.
13. Marco Chown Oved, Toby A.A. Heaps, Michael Yow. "The High Cost of Low Corporate Tax Rates," *Toronto Star*, December 14, 2017. https://projects.thestar.com/canadas-corporations-pay-less-tax-than-you-think.
14. Philippe Orfali, "Paradis fiscaux : plus de 380 milliards $ hors de portee, " *Le Journal de Quebec*, July 22, 2020. https://www.journaldequebec.com/2020/07/22/paradis-fiscaux-381-milliards--dactifs-a-labri-de-limpot.
15. Toby Sanger. "Time to step up for tax justice," *The Monitor*, November 1, 2019. https://www.policyalternatives.ca/publications/monitor/time-step-tax-justice.
16. Centre for International Corporate Tax Accountability and Research. *Tax Dodging by a Canadian Crown Corporation: Revera Living Making a Killing*. January 2021. https://cictar.org/wp-content/uploads/2021/01/Revera_Report_7-1.pdf.
17. Parliamentary Budget Officer, "Preliminary Findings on International Taxation," 2019. https://www.pbo-dpb.gc.ca/web/default/files/Documents/Reports/2019/Preliminary-Findings-International-Taxation/Report%20final.pdf.
18. Zach Dubinsky, "Wealthy Canadians hiding up to $240B abroad, CRA says," *CBC News*, June 28, 2018. https://www.cbc.ca/news/business/cra-tax-gap-foreign-holdings-1.4726983.
19. Harvey Cashore, Chelsea Gomez, and Gillian Findlay. "Trudeau's chief fundraiser linked to Cayman Islands tax scheme," *CBC News*, November 05, 2017. https://www.cbc.ca/news/business/stephen-bronfman-trudeau-paradise-papers-1.4382511.
20. Celebrity Net Worth. "How much is Frank Giustra Net Worth," https://www.celebritynetworth.com/richest-businessmen/richest-billionaires/frank-giustra-net-worth.
21. Anita Kumar, Marisa Taylor and Kevin G. Hall. "Inside Panama Papers: Multiple Clinton connections," *McClatchy Washington Bureau*, April 16, 2016. https://www.mcclatchydc.com/news/politics-government/election/article72215012.html.
22. Zach Dubinsky, "Panama Papers spur billion-dollar global tax windfall, with $15M found in Canada," *CBC News*, April 3, 2019. https://www.cbc.ca/news/politics/panama-papers-cra-tax-recovered-charges-1.5082058.
23. Alex Ballingall, "Canada audited $450B in international money transfers. Could there really have been none that broke the rules?" *Toronto Star*, November 25, 2020. https://www.thestar.com/politics/federal/2020/11/25/canada-audited-450b-in-international-money-transfers-could-there-really-have-been-none-that-broke-the-rules.html.
24. Philippe Orfali, "Paradis fiscaux : plus de 380 milliards $ hors de portee, " *Le Journal de Quebec*, July 22, 2020. https://www.journaldequebec.com/2020/07/22/paradis-fiscaux-381-milliards--dactifs-a-labri-de-limpot.
25. Christopher Knaus, "Tax office may apply 40% tax against multinationals for diverting profits," *The Guardian*, April 5, 2019. https://www.theguardian.com/australia-news/2019/apr/05/tax-office-may-apply-40-tax-against-multinationals-for-diverting-profits

26. Zach Dubinsky, "As U.K. moves to shut down tax-haven secrecy, Canada seen lagging," *CBC News*, May 1, 2018. https://www.cbc.ca/news/world/british-tax-havens-new-legislation-passed-1.4644172.
27. Toby Sanger. "Time to step up for tax justice," *The Monitor*, November 1, 2019. https://www.policyalternatives.ca/publications/monitor/time-step-tax-justice.
28. European Commission, "Fighting Tax Evasion and Avoidance: A year of progress," December 15, 2013. https://ec.europa.eu/commission/presscorner/detail/fr/MEMO_13_1096.
29. Murray Rankin, "Bill C-362 and 'Tax Fairness': Closing loopholes and bringing money back to Canada," *Broadbent Institute Blog*, December 13, 2017. https://www.broadbentinstitute.ca/murrayrankinndp/bill_c_362_and_tax_fairness_closing_loopholes_and_bringing_money_back_to_canada.
30. Parliamentary Budget Officer. "Deny deduction for transactions with foreign subsidiaries without any economic substance," October 11, 2019. https://www.pbo-dpb.gc.ca/web/default/files/Documents/ElectionProposalCosting/Results/33205650_EN.pdf.
31. Parliamentary Budget Officer. "Increased investment in tax compliance and enforcement," October 11, 2019. https://www.pbo-dpb.gc.ca/web/default/files/Documents/ElectionProposalCosting/Results/33205808_EN.pdf.
32. Parliamentary Budget Officer. "Estimating the return of additional federal spending on business tax compliance," October 08, 2020. https://www.pbo-dpb.gc.ca/web/default/files/Documents/Reports/RP-2021-026-S/RP-2021-026-S_en.pdf.
33. Marco Chown Oved and Robert Cribb, "Finance Minister Bill Morneau vows to close 'unfair' tax loopholes," *The Hamilton Spectator*, May 26, 2017. https://www.thespec.com/news/canada/2017/05/26/finance-minister-bill-morneau-vows-to-close-unfair-tax-loopholes.html.

Chapter 8

1. See the Broadbent Institute Tax Index: https://www.broadbentinstitute.ca/tax-index.
2. Marco Chown Oved, Toby A.A. Heaps, Michael Yow. "The High Cost of Low Corporate Tax Rates," *Toronto Star*, December 14, 2017. https://projects.thestar.com/canadas-corporations-pay-less-tax-than-you-think.
3. Ibid.
4. Finance Canada. "Marginal Effective Tax Rates Backgrounder," July 2019. https://www.canada.ca/en/department-finance/news/2019/07/backgrounder--marginal-effective-tax-rates.html.
5. Marco Chown Oved, Toby A.A. Heaps, Michael Yow. "The High Cost of Low Corporate Tax Rates," *Toronto Star*, December 14, 2017. https://projects.thestar.com/canadas-corporations-pay-less-tax-than-you-think.
6. Canadians for Tax Fairness, "Make Taxes More Progressive," 2019. https://www.taxfairness.ca/en/news/make-taxes-more-progressive.
7. Marco Chown Oved, Toby A.A. Heaps, Michael Yow. "The High Cost of Low Corporate Tax Rates," *Toronto Star*, December 14, 2017. https://projects.thestar.com/canadas-corporations-pay-less-tax-than-you-think.

8. Ibid.
9. Armine Yalnizyan, "Five reasons to say no to more corporate tax cuts," *The Globe and Mail*, January 28, 2011. https://www.theglobeandmail.com/report-on-business/economy/economy-lab/five-reasons-to-say-no-to-more-corporate-tax-cuts/article611285.
10. Ibid.
11. Pete Evans, "Every $1 spent on early childhood education pays back $6 later, report finds," *CBC News*, October 27, 2017. https://www.cbc.ca/news/business/early-childhood-education-1.4374820.
12. Marco Chown Oved, Toby A.A. Heaps, Michael Yow. "The High Cost of Low Corporate Tax Rates," *Toronto Star*, December 14, 2017. https://projects.thestar.com/canadas-corporations-pay-less-tax-than-you-think.
13. Ibid.
14. OECD. "Statutory corporate income tax rate," 2020. https://stats.oecd.org/index.aspx?DataSetCode=Table_II1.
15. Parliamentary Budget Officer. "Corporate Income Tax Rate Increase," October 11, 2019. https://www.pbo-dpb.gc.ca/web/default/files/Documents/ElectionProposalCosting/Results/32629642_EN.pdf.
16. Edward Helmore, "Amazon third-quarter earnings soar as pandemic sales triple profits," *The Guardian*, October 29, 2020. https://www.theguardian.com/technology/2020/oct/29/amazon-profits-latest-earnings-report-third-quarter-pandemic.
17. Isabelle Kirkwood, "Shopify doubles GMV, reports record profit in third-quarter results," *Betakit*, October 29, 2020. https://betakit.com/shopify-doubles-gmv-reports-record-profit-in-third-quarter-results/#:~:text=The%20e%2Dcommerce%20giant's%20revenue,a%20new%20record%20for%20Shopify.
18. Richard M. Bird. "Government Finance," in *Historical Studies of Canada*. https://www150.statcan.gc.ca/n1/pub/11-516-x/sectionh/4057752-eng.htm#1.
19. Alex Hemingway, "Excess profits tax needed to prevent profiteering amid COVID-19," Policy Note, April 9, 2020. https://www.policynote.ca/profits-tax.
20. Jonathan Nicholson, "Tax 'excess' profits of big money-making companies to fix coronavirus economy, scholar urges," *Market Watch*, April 30, 2020. https://www.marketwatch.com/story/tax-excess-profits-of-big-money-making-companies-to-fix-coronavirus-economy-scholar-urges-2020-04-30.
21. Bruce Anderson and David Coletto, "Wealth tax? Canadians like the idea." *Abacus Data*, November 19, 2020. https://abacusdata.ca/wealth-tax-canada-poll.

Chapter 9

1. Fair Tax Mark. *The Silicon Six and their $100 billion global tax gap*. December 2019. https://fairtaxmark.net/wp-content/uploads/2019/12/Silicon-Six-Report-5-12-19.pdf.
2. Matthew Gardner, "Amazon in Its Prime: Doubles Profits, Pays $0 in Federal Income Taxes," *Institute on Taxation and Economic Policy*, February 13, 2019. https://itep.org/amazon-in-its-prime-doubles-profits-pays-0-in-federal-income-taxes.
3. Innovation, Science and Economic Development Canada. *Canada's Communica-*

tions Future: Time to Act, Final Report of the Broadcasting and Telecommunications Legislative Review, January 2020. https://www.ic.gc.ca/eic/site/110.nsf/vwapj/BTLR_Eng-V3.pdf/$file/BTLR_Eng-V3.pdf, p. 122-123.
4. Friends of Canadian Broadcasting. "How Ottawa Subsidizes Junk News," September 5, 2019. https://friends.ca/explore/article/how-ottawa-subsidizes-junk-news.
5. Alex Ballingall, "Google and Facebook got growing share of federal ad dollars after Justin Trudeau took power," *Toronto Star*, January 11, 2021. https://www.thestar.com/politics/federal/2021/01/11/google-and-facebook-got-growing-share-of-federal-ad-dollars-after-justin-trudeau-took-power.html.
6. Innovation, Science and Economic Development Canada. *Canada's Communications Future: Time to Act*, Final Report of the Broadcasting and Telecommunications Legislative Review, January 2020. https://www.ic.gc.ca/eic/site/110.nsf/vwapj/BTLR_Eng-V3.pdf/$file/BTLR_Eng-V3.pdf.
7. Friends of Canadian Broadcasting. "How Ottawa Subsidizes Junk News," September 5, 2019. https://friends.ca/explore/article/how-ottawa-subsidizes-junk-news.
8. Canadians for Tax Fairness, "Level the Digital Playing Field – Fact Sheet," October 9, 2019. https://www.taxfairness.ca/sites/default/files/factsheets/digital_fact_sheet.pdf.
9. Tom Blackwell, "'Working conditions are hell': Amazon employees not surprised its warehouses have seen hundreds of COVID cases," *National Post*, December 23, 2020. https://nationalpost.com/news/canada/working-conditions-are-hell-amazon-employees-not-surprised-its-warehouses-have-seen-hundreds-of-covid-cases.
10. Livia Albeck-Ripka, "Australia Moves to Force Google and Facebook to Compensate Media Outlets," *The New York Times*, April 20, 2020. https://www.nytimes.com/2020/04/20/business/media/australia-facebook-google.html.
11. Leigh Thomas, "France orders tech giants to pay digital tax," *Reuters*, November 25, 2020. https://www.reuters.com/article/us-france-usa-tax/france-orders-tech-giants-to-pay-digital-tax-idUKKBN28522M.
12. Parliamentary Budget Officer, "Taxation of large technology companies," September 29, 2019. https://www.pbo-dpb.gc.ca/web/default/files/Documents/ElectionProposalCosting/Results/32977970_EN.pdf.

Chapter 10

1. Finance Canada. *Fall Economic Statement 2020*: https://www.budget.gc.ca/fes-eea/2020/report-rapport/toc-tdm-en.html.
2. See Chapter 5 in Linda McQuaig, *Sport and Prey of Capitalists*. Dundurn Press, 2019.
3. Ibid, p.143.

Chapter 11

1. Canadian Centre for Policy Alternatives. *New Decade, New Deal: Our plan for a just and sustainable economy*. 2020 Alternative Federal Budget.